TIMES AND SEASONS

*Creating transformative worship
throughout the year*

Richard Giles

Music resource notes
Riyehee Hong

Photographs
Walter Davis

CHURCH PUBLISHING
an imprint of
Church Publishing Incorporated, New York

ISBN-13: 978-0-89869-613-4

A catalog record of this title is available from the Library of Congress.

First published in the United Kingdom by SCM-Canterbury Press.

First published in the United States by

Church Publishing, Incorporated
445 Fifth Avenue
New York, New York 10016

www.churchpublishing.com

Printed in the United Kingdom.

5   4   3   2   1

Times and Seasons

CONTENTS

For the cathedral community at Philadelphia, a people
who walk the walk

and for Christine Smith,
a publisher who never gives up

INTRODUCTION

One of the great gifts of the mainstream liturgical churches to the rest of the Christian family is the Church's Year: the annual cycle of liturgical observances by which the salient points in the life and saving work of Jesus the Christ are brought to the forefront of the minds of the faithful. In one sense, every day the Christian wakes to is a celebration of the mystery of Christ's death and resurrection, but we are poor, weak creatures for whom, in our own journey, birthdays and anniversaries are essential milestones on the sometimes endless path, at which we can pause to give thanks, to reflect, and to celebrate.

In our spiritual journey too we need milestones to mark out our unmade and sometimes winding road into the impenetrable mystery of all that God in Christ, 'reconciling the world to himself', has done for us. 'Human kind cannot bear very much reality,' wrote T. S. Eliot, and the Church's Year opens up a route for us, well trodden and repeatable, by which we may draw near to the cloud and glimpse the glory. Otherwise it is simply too much for us.

The first followers of Jesus soon developed a weekly cycle of remembrance, with the first working day of the week (Sunday) marking the resurrection, and that three days previous (Friday) the crucifixion. Fast and feast gave a rhythm to each seven-day period. Fairly soon afterwards, and not surprisingly given their familiarity with the calendar of Hebrew festivals, Christians augmented the weekly cycle with an annual one incorporating all the significant events in the story of their Lord, from conception to glorification.

For good measure, the lives of the most illustrious followers of Jesus are also marked by an annual remembrance, usually on the anniversary of their death (understood as a birth into eternal life).

Instead of one unbroken and featureless plateau in which one Sunday is very much like another, all churches holding to some degree of liturgical awareness present the worshipper with a continual series of troughs and hills to enliven the journey through the yearly cycle. These obstacles to a quiet and easy life can sometimes require perseverance and determination, but they certainly relieve the boredom, and if scaling the hills is sometimes hard going, the view from the top makes it all worthwhile.

The liturgical year is a series of feasts and fasts, of joyous celebration preceded by periods of penitential preparation, in which the two great festivals of Christmas and Easter are the twin liturgical peaks. In Western culture these two 'holidays' continue also to serve as milestones of any secular year. Other festivals such as Pentecost, though less prominent in the popular mind, also have theological and liturgical significance. The year traditionally begins on Advent Sunday, four weeks before Christmas, with a period of preparation for the coming of Christ, both in his birth and at the end of time.

After a post-Christmas lull, the penitential season of Lent begins the long slow haul up to Easter. Whereas the date of Christmas is fixed, the timing of Easter is lunar, linked as it is to the Jewish observance of Passover. The dating of Easter serves to fill many charts and tables, and is something of a nuisance, but generally keeps the world guessing and the Church on its toes.

Easter itself is of course not the observance of a single day, but a liturgical party lasting 50 days, culminating in the Christian feast of Pentecost, celebrating the coming of the Holy Spirit on the Church. After Trinity Sunday (kept on the first Sunday after Pentecost), the long stream of Sundays when nothing much is happening, and green vestments are worn, begins, until it's Advent Sunday once again.

These long green weeks pose something of a problem of nomenclature. Until the recent period of liturgical reform, these Sundays were numbered as 'Sundays after Pentecost' in the Roman Church, while the Church of England, following the pre-Reformation Sarum Use, preferred 'Sundays after Trinity'. Both these were misleading, according the feasts of Pentecost and of the Holy Trinity a significance that liturgically they did not possess. With Vatican II the Roman Church came up with the term 'Sundays in Ordinary Time' which is far more sensible, but for some reason resisted by other liturgical churches, perhaps because they didn't think of it first. The Church of England has even gone back to 'after Trinity' in *Common Worship* (2000) after having flirted with 'after Pentecost' in the *Alternative Service Book 1980*. This puts it out of step with the Episcopal Church, which adopted 'after Pentecost' in its 1979 Prayer Book revision.

Whatever the quirks of individual liturgical commissions or committees, we have in the liturgical year a great treasure. Through it, the worshipper is invited, not simply to note or to observe, but to participate in a re-living of past events by which the Christian story is preserved and reinvigorated. The Church's Year provides the code by which the worshipper is able to access past events as present reality.

The Church's Year is observed and celebrated in rituals and customs which in many cases go back to the very first centuries of Christian history, but in others represent accretions gradually added as time has gone by. As in any living tradition, the way we do things will be a mixture of ancient customs and modern adaptations to a changing world. Evolution is in the end the only evidence of life with any chance of survival.

Common Worship: Times and Seasons (2006) is an invaluable resource from the Church of England with which to enrich the language of our yearly cycle of liturgical observance, but in the final analysis words are not enough. Nowhere more than in liturgy does the old adage ring true: 'actions speak louder than words'. We need in addition to the texts practical ideas for bringing the words to life. Amid the plethora of new liturgical texts and supplementary material which have swamped most sections of the Western Church in the last half century, how might we continue to bring the Church's Year to life, using both ancient tradition and newly minted insights from contemporary experience?

We need to count our blessings in this regard, especially those of us in England of the Anglican tradition. It concentrates the liturgical mind to recall that, a little over one hundred years ago, Parliament, not the Church, was the final court of appeal on matters liturgical, and as late as 1871 the Judicial Committee of the Privy Council decreed that the priest taking the eastward position at the altar, and the wearing of eucharistic vestments, were illegal (Bell, 1952). Such nonsense soon demanded radical change, but not before several clergy has been imprisoned for infringing the provisions of the Public Worship Regulation Act 1874.

These seem incredible stories, spun from an era in church history already inconceivable to us in our generation. We have come a long way in 140 years, and now enjoy, despite continuing wide differences in theological emphasis and worship style, an approach to worship which is unselfconsciously visual and tactile.

Common Worship: Times and Seasons (2006) is a concrete expression of the discovery by the whole Church that when we come to worship God we are all in some sense 'ritualists'. This is not because we have all gone 'High Church' (to use a quaint outmoded phrase), but because we have all stumbled upon the value of colour, and touch, and movement, and drama in worship, and of a 'procedure regularly followed' (which is what the dictionary tells us ritual is). No matter how hard we may try, we are creatures of habit constrained by our own predictability; ritualists every one.

The pages that follow will explore a few possibilities for each liturgical season, suggesting simple and accessible ways in which we may mark the distinctive character of each section of our journey and celebrate the difference in eucharistic worship.

Whatever the time or the season, orders of service tailor-made for the occasion should always be preferred to hymnals and prayer books, for reasons both liturgical and evangelistic. An order of service, which contains within a few pages everything the worshipper will need, can by its layout and design convey the whole mood and purpose of the season. It guarantees easy participation, eliminating all surplus material and, by omitting the text of prayers or readings, encourages the worshipper to engage in the dialogue of liturgy rather than spending the entire time with one's nose buried in a book.

Throughout all this, our worship from beginning to end should above all be natural yet dignified, restrained yet Spirit-filled, spontaneous yet ordered, of the moment yet timeless. It is interesting to note the observations of Bishop Hensley Henson upon witnessing worship in the Church in Sweden in 1920:

> I was struck by the *naturalness* of the service. There was a complete absence of the fussy self-consciousness which disfigures our ceremonial functions in England . . . our clergy in vestments move with the awkward concern of a *nouveau riche* in the drawing room. (Henson, 1946, vol. 2, p. 41)

Henson attributed this liturgical malaise to the fact that, in his view, medieval practice had been *continued* in the Church in Sweden, but *revived* in the Church of England, an assertion which is worth a robust challenge. Fortunately we have improved since the 1920s (or gone on more trips to Sweden), and today Anglican worship is noted, especially in its cathedrals, for splendid unfussy ceremonial and worship of noble simplicity. Let this always be our aim, wherever we attempt to offer liturgical worship as the work of the people of God.

1 ORDINARY TIME

Ordinary Time: seating arrangement

The first thought in putting together any material tracing the cycle of the liturgical year is to begin with Advent Sunday, when our annual journey begins all over again. In this case, however, it is important first to establish the norm, the regular, the unexceptional, from which we will sally forth to begin a special season, observe a fast, or celebrate a feast as something different, special and remarkable. In mountaineering terms, ordinary time is the col, the shoulder, of the mountain, the place for a strategic high camp from which the summit can be assailed and to which in due course we can gratefully return to restore our strength.

Characteristics

Not that any Sunday is 'ordinary' of course. Whenever the community of faith gathers to make eucharist under the Spirit of God, we can expect extraordinary things to happen. Our liturgical celebrations, no matter how carefully planned or well ordered, should always be approached in humility and with respect, for we can never be sure what will break forth from such a dynamic as the coming of the Spirit on the living Body of Christ which is the Church. We shall do our best always to do everything 'decently and in order' (1 Corinthians 14.40), but we should never delude ourselves into thinking we are totally in charge.

Those who plan and lead worship are not merely 'events organizers' or 'party managers', but agents of God's transforming power, like the servants at the wedding at Cana. They simply did what was asked of them, putting in position the raw material through which God would reveal his glory in the person and ministry of Jesus (John 2.1–11). They did not demur or dismiss or complain, and so became midwives of wondrous change. When we gather to celebrate in the presence of Christ in our own generation, we too must allow the unexpected initiative of God to burst through the ordinary, the predictable and the unlikely. If we simply do what is asked of us, demanding nothing but expecting everything, we shall be faithful stewards of the mysteries of God, and witnesses of the transforming work of he who makes all things new.

Sundays in Ordinary Time are in one sense 'leftover Sundays' between Pentecost (or Trinity) and Advent, and also (depending on whose calendar we are keeping) between Epiphany and Lent. They are the Sundays when nothing particular is happening, and when we can settle down to enjoy the regular routine. Green is worn as the liturgical colour, expressive of creation, and this becomes the 'background' colour of the whole liturgical year. Like the foliage we use to set off flower arrangements to best advantage, greenery is beautiful in its own right, but usually plays second fiddle to the blooms which dominate the display.

Cultural context

Sundays in Ordinary Time are, however, of immense significance in their own right in establishing what the Church is really like, week in week out. These are the Sundays when we are most ourselves, and when we can be most hospitable and embracing. These 'ordinary' Sundays are the times we really need our visitors to show up and join us, rather than those special occasions like Midnight Mass or the Easter

Vigil when everything is so exceptional and untypical and we hardly have time to say 'hello' let alone introduce or explain.

Choreography

How can we honour the role of a Sunday in Ordinary Time, doing justice to the various facets of its nature, in such a way that the faithful are nurtured and energized and the newcomer engaged and welcomed?

The question of how we might design and lead worship which engages, inspires and transforms is addressed fully in *Creating Uncommon Worship* (Giles, 2004a), but here we need only note that it will be on the ordinary green Sundays of the Church's life that such liturgy will be at its most telling and effective. This is indeed the supreme work of the people of God: to offer such an experience of worship that we will be stopped in our tracks and glimpse, here in our midst, nothing less than the glory of God.

This book is concerned primarily with feasts and fasts, but nevertheless it will be worthwhile briefly to examine what might be described as everyday fare, so that we might appreciate the special banquets even more.

Setting

The liturgical space in which the assembly gathers needs to be re-examined meticulously and with fresh eyes. In what ways does it inspire and enable? In what ways does it frustrate and inhibit? Is there a pinch point at which it gets in the way of everything we are trying to say and to become? Can we adapt or rearrange our church building(s) to facilitate more effectively the kind of worship experience we wish to offer, and the necessary hospitality that should flow naturally from it?

These questions are addressed fully in *Re-Pitching the Tent* (Giles, 2004b), which includes both a theological rationale and a detailed design guide for taking hold of our liturgical spaces and giving them a good shake.

For a faith community to enter fully into the cycle of the seasons of the Church's liturgical year, it will need above all a liturgical space that allows dramatic change between one season and another, in which flexibility of spatial arrangement will be of primary importance. Like the stage of a theatre, a liturgical space that is serving its community well will be one which, by its flexibility, versatility and neutrality, can create a number of very different scenes each conveying a totally different world.

All too often, the interior of the building that is our liturgical space will, instead of providing the means by which many scenes are set, take centre stage itself, dominating and constricting everything we do, demanding the central role. As a result, our liturgical experience is, as Lady Macbeth would have said, 'cabin'd, cribb'd, confin'd'. We have forgotten the primary purpose of the church building, and have awarded it the status of a sacred temple when all the time it was supposed to be a provisional tent, sheltering the people of God gathered for worship.

All is not lost, however, and the process of unlocking our cluttered church buildings and opening them up to become appropriate liturgical spaces for today is a constant work in progress. To take one example, the liturgical space at Philadelphia Cathedral was redesigned in 2002 to make the most of the basic basilican plan of the building, which had been obscured by the furnishing of the interior in unbridled high Victorian gothic, and by the riotous decoration of every wall surface.

The renovated space establishes a level stone floor throughout the nave and narthex, to provide a spacious and uncluttered 'liturgical pavement' upon which the three liturgical foci of baptismal pool, ambo and altar table can stand in noble simplicity. Each of the three foci have ample space around them to form true gathering places for the assembly.

The floor plan places the ambo at the west end, facing east, the altar table at the east end, and the baptismal font in the unusually wide south aisle. The font was placed there for practical reasons, but the configuration of the three foci was later found to resemble closely the layout typical of the Syrian Orthodox tradition. All three liturgical foci stand on the liturgical pavement of the nave, open and accessible to the people of God, without intervening step, rail or screen.

At the far east end of the liturgical space, up three steps from the nave, is the *presbyterium* occupying the site of the former choir chancel. This takes the form of a semi-circular stone bench at the centre of which is the bishop's chair (*cathedra*), in the pattern of the earliest known Christian basilicas, a few examples of which survive in Italy and Turkey. Thus in place of a high altar, distant from the people, we have the more primitive symbol of the presidency of the bishop. At Philadelphia the stone bench of the *presbyterium* has been continued right around the perimeter walls of the cathedral's interior, so that symbolically the assembly of the baptized sits 'alongside' the bishop as fellow ministers of the Church of God.

Orientation

The single most important question in designing a room where the assembly can make eucharist is the seating plan. How can the assembly be gathered in such a way that their very configuration gives eloquent expression to the nature of their life together in Christ? This issue should take first place before bothering our heads about where we place the font and how we design the altar table; it is fundamental to our self-awareness as a community of ministers of the liturgy.

The details hardly matter – there is no 'right' or 'wrong' way – but God loves a cheerful try-er, and making the attempt is the thing. To make the connection between a seating plan and a healthy theology of the assembly participating in ministry, the seating needs to be in some form of configuration which speaks of gathering around to take part rather than passively watching. Such a configuration might be antiphonal (facing one another across a central axis), semi circular, or on three sides of a square. Almost any old plan will do, provided it rescues us from the serried ranks of seats (whether pews or chairs) all facing in one direction, where from the safety of their liturgical bunker, the worshipper peers out at the chosen few performing the liturgical show.

It is therefore essential that the seating plan of the assembly in Ordinary Time establishes the bench mark of our liturgical praxis – our 'Greenwich Mean Time' of communal life. From this norm everything we do in observing fasts and celebrating feasts, every seasonal variation, will flow naturally.

Seating plans expressive of communal participation in liturgy are not therefore for 'special occasions only', but are the norm of our liturgical existence, our 'ordinary' everyday mode. There can be no turning back to our bad old habits of sitting in classroom mode; it is no longer an option for us to revert to being a passive audience, for we have tasted the fruits of liturgy as a shared enterprise, in which all minister and all receive.

Presidency

Intrinsically bound up with the seating of the assembly is the seating for the president and other ministers of the eucharist. In this context 'ministers of the eucharist' refers to all those who lead worship, lay or ordained; who sit in a distinct place, and whose particular role is denoted by some form of distinctive dress, most probably a plain white alb reminiscent of the baptismal robe of all the faithful.

Soon after the first few centuries, Christian ordained leadership became clericalized, hierarchical and exclusive. In spatial terms, the leadership withdrew into another room (the 'sanctuary') where from behind a screen it conducted worship in a new variation of the Old Covenant's holy of holies, while the assembly, excluded from the action, either milled around or gazed forward hopefully, occasionally alerted by the ringing of a bell to the most solemn moments when their full attention was demanded.

The Church today, in seeking to renew its liturgy, has sixteen hundred years of clericalism to undo, and there is no better place to begin than by bringing the president and the other ministers of the eucharist out of liturgical purdah to take their rightful place once again in the midst of the people as members of the assembly along with everyone else.

It will of course always remain the case that the president needs a good vantage point to see and be seen. There is no need to play 'hunt the president' every Sunday morning, and the president's chair should be located with much care and thought, with priority given to putting behind us for ever any suggestion of exclusive privilege or pre-eminence.

Instead the emphasis will be on the president emerging from the assembly to lead his/her fellow pilgrims along the road. Here set before us is that precious and rare gift: the servant leader, in whom servanthood and authority are at work in equal measure. This is the kind of leadership exhorted by and modelled by Jesus himself, combining clear and decisive authority with self-emptying love, neither autocratic not subservient. It is a tall order for us, but we can start by seating the president in the assembly as if this is the kind of leadership we want to be blessed with, and to express in our liturgical gathering.

Making music

Alongside the question of how we seat the assembly, it can safely be said that music is the single most important characteristic by which we can discern the priorities, purpose and self-understanding of a community of faith and where it is on its journey. Music is the dead give-away. In terms of the renewal of the liturgy it is absolutely vital to get music right, and to take endless pains in doing so.

This means moving away once and for all from music as performance to an understanding of music as a means of transformation. This will be bad news for snooty organists who turn their noses up at anything written after 1900 and, with total disregard for what is appropriate or helpful, attempt to reproduce the repertoire of a cathedral choir with a complement of three septuagenarians and a token child.

In contrast, a director of music whose primary concern is the liturgy will understand that the assembly is the choir, who together must be helped, loved and cajoled into making music. In so doing they will discover that they are not, after all, tone deaf, or musically challenged, and will surprise themselves with the powerful and moving effect they can produce, and the fun and satisfaction they can get from doing so. Those with particular gifts, whether as singers or musicians, will of course have a special part to play, but they will do so as enablers of all, not specialists who disenfranchise the whole.

Many a project for liturgical reordering comes a cropper on the rocks of how and where to seat those who lead the assembly in music-making. Our current woes are due mainly to the Victorian fondness for replacing the parish orchestra – composed of a variety of instruments perched up in a west gallery – with a single instrument, the pipe organ, accompanying a group of singers dressed up in robes and occupying a prominent place of honour in the chancel.

This both unionized and clericalized music-making, creating a quasi-monastic body of liturgical ministers strategically placed between the people in the nave and the priest in the sanctuary. Having once gained these heights, robed choirs are usually extremely reluctant to relinquish hard-won territory, no matter how unsuitable their restricted location for the work they are supposed to do. They have also developed a taste for processing in and out, the assembly standing in deference, and can be as demanding as a prima donna with regard to their dressing-room facilities.

We can but begin again with a whole new approach which recognizes the assembly as the choir, and what we used to call the choir as those highly valued members of the assembly with special gifts in music-making with which they can help the rest of us to reach our potential. Seen in this light, there really is no problem. The singers are reunited with the assembly, where they truly belong, and in which integrated location their special seating and special robes no longer have relevance. Like the *schola* of a monastic community, the singers emerge from, and re-emerge with, the rest of the community as and when required to play their part.

Movement

One of the most significant developments in what might be called renewed or 'progressive' liturgy is the rediscovery that the assembly at worship is a community of pilgrims on the move.

This movement may take the form of a solemn procession, a straggle of travellers singing a song, or even a troupe of dancers stepping out with joy. The method and style of getting from liturgical A to B will depend very much on the faith community, reflecting its character, way of doing things, and mood. The main thing is for us not to get stuck in 'the way we always do it here', but to ring the changes and to have fun finding our own way.

Liturgical dance, if and when we incorporate it, should mean only one thing: the dance of the whole community, not a performance by the few for the many. In an assembly come of age, the specialism of 'liturgical dancer' should become as redundant as that of 'chalice-bearer', for among the people of God all dance or no one does.

The president goes ahead, leading the pilgrim band, seeking out the place where the community can safely rest and feed on God's pasture. The normal ecclesiastic precedence of senior cleric taking up the rear is superseded by the need to model the faithful shepherd and guide on a journey that is in itself sacramental, the few short steps being an outward and visible sign of the inward and spiritual grace of a lifetime's journeying under God.

Liturgical furniture

The three foci of every liturgical assembly – font, ambo and altar table – should be reassessed and their location in the liturgical space re-examined by every community of faith engaged in liturgical renewal.

First will come the task of reducing the number of liturgical foci to three. In the vast majority of worship spaces inherited from previous generations we shall find at least two of everything, often three or four. Rationalizing these into three workable and meaningful foci for bath, book and bread is a formative experience for any faith community as we recall our history, determine what speaks to us today, and face up to decisions about what to keep, what to discard, or perhaps what to combine.

This process is not necessarily one of sweeping away the past; far from it. There are many situations when we can reuse furniture of good quality, though not necessarily for the purpose originally intended. Many are the pulpits which, cut down to a manageable size and dethroned from their pediment, make excellent ambos, and many the altar rails which, skillfully reworked, begin a new career as panels to encase a new altar table or even a baptismal pool.

It is fair to say, however, that furniture of outstanding quality, which we must move heaven and earth to incorporate in a renovated liturgical space, is the exception rather than the rule. All too often unsuitable furniture is retained for nostalgic reasons or to calm down potential objectors, with sorry end results.

Unless the old furniture really is outstanding, it is better to begin again. As a group exercise thrash out what you as a community want the liturgical foci to *say*, and then find artists and craftspeople (preferably local) who will help you translate the desired effect into physical structures that will do justice to your community's identity and aspirations.

The altar table is the liturgical focus that dominates most liturgical spaces, and remains a powerful symbol of Christ among us. As the people of God draw near to the altar table in liturgies freed from restrictive clericalism, the shape of the altar table itself will achieve greater significance.

The altar table is now the liturgical focus around which the assembly gathers in new-found confidence, thanking God for 'making us worthy to stand here before you'. As we all group ourselves around the altar table with sleeves rolled up, it is seen as work bench rather than symbolic monument.

The familiar long rectangle, more reminiscent of a sideboard than a table, should gracefully bow out and give way to a square, or even circular, altar table, at which there is no 'front or back' (or even 'north end' or 'south end' if one is ancient enough to remember), only a table around which we gather to do our work and lay out the gifts of all that we have and all that we are.

The Sunday Liturgy

The Sunday Liturgy in Ordinary Time should lay the ground work for all that follows at other times and in other seasons by incorporating and making explicit all the components that characterize the life and work of our community of faith.

Elements of worship

Whatever our local situation, there are a number of elements common to all communities where liturgical renewal is being taken seriously, and to the liturgies they celebrate:

1 **Participation:** the assembly becomes engaged in the liturgical action, and mobilized for ministry. Even those who come intending merely to observe find themselves caught up in the liturgical offering of the community, and doing ministry before they realize it.

2 **Journey:** integral to this engagement in worship is the experience of journey, as the assembly, no longer staying put, passive and immobile, physically moves as a community of pilgrimage from place to place as the liturgy unfolds. As it does so, it focuses on different aspects of the liturgy: penitence and/or affirmation (font), formation through the Scriptures (ambo), and breaking bread (altar table).

3 **Physicality:** as the journey progresses, the tactile nature of the experience – walking, getting wet, touching others, being censed, handling holy things – means that worship can no longer remain cerebral or theoretical, or at arms length.

4 **Theological formation:** the participant in worship is taught, through the spoken word, through gesture and ritual, the nature of the community's life and of its work as the people of God. Theology informs the liturgy, and the liturgy makes

explicit what is happening, leading the participant into an ever deeper understanding (see below).

5 **Treasures new and old:** renewed liturgy will bring forth the best of both new and
old, honouring tradition but constantly renewing it. This will be particularly true
of music for the liturgy, which should always exhibit an extraordinary breadth of
styles and variety of sources, albeit with an emphasis on the creativity of our own
generation.

6 **Solemnity and joy:** worship will be at its best when it manages somehow to combine dignified solemnity with inexpressible joy always bursting through (or about
to). This echoes in word, ritual and song the 'noble simplicity' which the liturgical
space itself should always strive to express

Theological insights

In short, liturgy which is renewed takes what we have always known in theory but
rarely in practice, and makes it real and actual and here-and-now for every participant. Two examples will suffice:

1 The **centrality of baptism** is a concept the Church has long paid lip service to, but
not brought into play in weekly liturgical experience. In the United States, the
Book of Common Prayer (1979) of the Episcopal Church was predicated on a
rediscovered emphasis on baptismal covenant, but from the appearance of most
liturgical spaces one would never guess it. Sunday liturgies continue by and large
to ignore the font, which in most cases remains a bird bath in a corner and (to add
insult to injury) without water unless a baptism is pending.

   In response, let our Sunday Liturgy be an occasion when the whole assembly
gathers at the baptismal pool (or even round the bird bath if that's all we have
for the moment) and let us get wet, as we say sorry for making such a mess of our
baptismal promises and affirm our determination to do better at living them out.
After just a few weeks of this regular routine, the penny drops that the font is not
a dried-up redundant symbol in a corner, used once a lifetime, but a place where
the community gathers week by week to renew its life, and this because baptism
(not confirmation or ordination) is the anointing and commissioning that unites us
all.

2 The **transformation of priesthood** is part and parcel of the New Testament package but, as with baptism, is a concept that rarely sees the light of day in the regular
experience of Christian worship. Jesus Christ is revealed in the Christian Scriptures
as the new high priest who, replacing in his own person the Aaronic priesthood of

the Temple ritual, shares with the whole community of Christ's faithful the priestly task of intercession and reconciliation.

Deep-seated clericalism usually sees to it that such notions remain corralled in the realm of theory. Not only in the hierarchical churches of the Catholic tradition, but equally in the churches of the Reformation, the domination of the many by the few remains the norm of the worship experience for the vast majority of Christians.

Working out ways in which we might, at least symbolically, include the whole community in an experience of a shared priesthood is a primary task of liturgical renewal. How might what has previously been considered the preserve of the few be opened up to become the privilege of all? Five examples will suffice to indicate the way ahead, bearing in mind that there are many others yet to be discovered and explored:

1   **Mutual recognition:** at the entrance, once the president at the chair is ready to begin the liturgy, before a word is spoken, the president and other liturgical ministers should give a slow and solemn bow to each side of the assembly. This is a simple but effective way to indicate that all members of the assembly are regarded as fellow ministers of the eucharist.

2   **Reverencing the altar table:** at the entry of the ministers also, it has been customary in many traditions for the president and other ordained ministers to kiss the altar table. Why not invite, at least on special occasions, the whole community (for all are ministers of the eucharist) to enter in procession and do the same?

3   **Wearing the stole:** the stole has since earliest times been the symbol of the priestly office and as such jealously guarded by the ordained. Why might not the president, when others are about to lead the community of faith in reading, preaching, singing or praying, remove the stole and vest with it the person who will, at least for the next few minutes, address the assembly? In this way, individual ministers, lay or ordained, are empowered, authority is shared, and priesthood expanded to embrace many who minister in Christ's name.

4   **Praying the eucharistic prayer:** at the altar table during the eucharistic prayer, it is customary for the president to adopt the *orans* position of prayer, with arms extended. Why not invite the whole assembly, gathered around the altar, to do the same? This is a highly visual and powerfully symbolic way of affirming that all the baptized are co-celebrants of the eucharist.

5   **Sharing communion:** at communion we have grown accustomed to assuming that only those properly authorized may touch the sacred vessels and minister the sacrament to others. Why not initiate methods of sharing communion which make redundant nice definitions of worthiness and authorization? This might be done by

inviting all members of the assembly to come forward to take into their own hands the sacred vessels placed on the altar table, or to pass the sacrament one to another.

In all these things, we may at first feel shocked or even repelled, excited or transformed, but will in one way or another be brought face to face with the tactile before-our-very-eyes reality of the theological verities which the Church has always professed but rarely put into practice. In such gestures as these, which are tangible, understandable and accessible, we begin to reconnect with our theological roots and reclaim our spiritual birthright.

Preaching

The relationship between the preaching of the word and the preaching effected by the liturgy itself is a huge subject, and can only be touched upon here. The important thing, however, is to recognize that the liturgy can be its own proclamation of good news, in the spirit of Francis of Assisi, who is said to have preached the gospel simply by walking from one side of a town to the other, or of St Columba, who is said to have instructed St Aidan, sent off from Iona to Lindisfarne, 'preach the gospel; use words if you have to'.

In other words, the liturgy properly celebrated can be said to need no embellishment by way of additional words or commentary; as proclamation goes it is powerful enough in its own right. It can be a conversion experience, bearing fruit in lives turned round and renewed. We all know times – for example at a mass of the Last Supper on Maundy (Holy) Thursday – when the power of the liturgy can be so overpowering that to preach a homily seems an intrusive interruption not devoid of hubris. Let the liturgy speak for itself.

At the same time, Thomas Cranmer's practical wisdom was exhibited in his insistence that the word should be proclaimed every time the eucharist was celebrated. This was due not just to Reformation euphoria at the panacean power of the preached word. Cranmer was apparently as aware as we are that the experience of the average liturgy can be decidedly underwhelming, and may need help from an interpretive voice to nudge it along in the right direction, or lift it above the humdrum level of the vainly repetitious. The Sunday 8 a.m. eucharist, so beloved of those opting out of parish life in churches up and down England, would have died of natural causes long ago if a powerful challenging homily had consistently been made part of the menu as Cranmer insisted it should.

A persistent problem, however, is the prevailing confusion between a sermon and a homily. Although the dictionary makes little distinction between the two, in popular usage within the Church there is a world of difference. We tend to think of the homily as a contribution to the liturgy, whereas the sermon is seen as something that can stand alone, something around which an act of worship can be constructed. A sermon is a piece of work that can be filed away for future use or taped for the house-bound or even, in outstanding cases, collected into a book for publication.

By contrast, the homily is a work of preaching that knows its place as a component of the liturgy; it makes way for the greater good of the whole experience of a composite and many-faceted act of worship. The homily is there to serve, not parade itself. Given human characteristics, the homily is self-effacing, the sermon rather pleased with itself.

The sermon is too often an exercise in self-indulgence on the preacher's part, an opportunity to spout Greek and parade knowledge. In particular the sermon provides a field day for the etymologist, transforming what is ordinarily a harmless private pastime, interesting enough if trapped in one's study on a rainy afternoon, into a public spectacle capable of seriously and permanently damaging the hearer's spiritual health.

The homilist has no regard for preachers who file sermons away for future use, or who complain that changes in the lectionary will wreak havoc with their habit of recycling their written texts. The homily has relevance only for a particular liturgical and historical moment. The proper place for a homily, once the liturgy for which it was created is over, is the waste-paper basket.

As the pastor theologian W. H. Vanstone put it:

> so the sermon has done its work when it has been preached and offered. The preacher, having prepared it with the greatest care, will now destroy the script or erase it from his memory; for the occasion of this particular offering will not recur, and if the same should be preached again there would then be no cost involved in it, and therefore no offering. (Beeson, 2006)

Whereas the sermon is likely to take the form of a full manuscript occupying (too) many typed sheets of A4, the homily may consist merely of a few headings written in longhand on the kind of scraps of paper you keep in the kitchen drawer to make shopping lists on. The homily has no pretensions to literary greatness. Indeed, in some cases it may not exist in written form at all, emerging straight from the heart and mind of the preacher extempore.

The homily will be delivered as often from the chair, the president seated, as from the ambo, or by the preacher moving about the assembly. Remaining seated to address the assembly changes the dynamic of preaching in an interesting and powerful way. It demands a certain intimacy of scale (an assembly seated no more than, say, ten rows deep), and reasonable visibility, but given these, it moves us from the arena of the lecture to that of the small seminar group. I am reminded every time of the compline addresses we received every Friday night at theological college; the high-light of the week in terms of the imparting of spiritual insight and wisdom.

There is much to be said for the idea that only extempore preaching, by the preacher soaked in the Scriptures and the liturgy of the Church, is true preaching; all the rest is the reading of essays. Extempore preaching requires not long hours in the study with a Greek Testament, but long hours of prayerful preparation learning the 'mind of Christ' which Paul asserts is ours (1 Corinthians 2.16). To make time to be still for a whole hour at some point before the liturgy begins, having mulled over the readings throughout the previous week, should be sufficient to enable any preacher alive in the Spirit to speak with insight and with power of the things of God to the people of God.

It sounds scary stuff, but only because we have pampered ourselves too long with the props of full texts, quotation books and Greek lexicons. Let us let go and let us preach. 'Always be ready', we read in 1 Peter 3.15, 'to make your defence to anyone who demands from you an accounting for the hope that is in you.' The ability and the readiness to do so should be part and parcel of the skill set of all Christians, even more so of those ordained to the work of ministry.

Trevor Beeson relates how Archbishop Randall Davidson encountered a preacher who, having once preached an extempore sermon to much acclaim, had sworn never to preach from a text again. Dismayed by what he heard, he declared, 'I Randall Davidson, by Divine permission Primate of All England and Metropolitan, do here-by release you from your vow' (Beeson, 2002). Faced with the turgid book-bound preaching of the Church today, especially as encountered in the United States, one likes to think the good Archbishop would have hurriedly adapted his dispensation to instead release the preacher from the obligation of ever again having to write out a sermon in full.

Of course the sermon, with every sentence carefully constructed and every word typed out, will remain necessary for those grand occasions when our knees knock and our stomachs rumble, especially on occasions when we may get quoted and in a none too friendly way. For all regular preaching however, by a pastor at home among his/her flock, the homily preached from some basic headings is the appropriate response to the privilege of being authorized to preach the good news in the context of the liturgy. To insert a sermon in this situation is usually a practice revealing a lack of understanding of what liturgical preaching is about, and not devoid of the urge to show off learning or cleverness with words. To read a sermon of this kind in the context of liturgy is the work of clergy who cannot escape their theological college or seminary. They declaim sermons which may have impressed their professor of homiletics in the context of a seminar, but cut no ice with the assembly of the faithful.

When the assembly meets to make eucharist, it meets to be fed, to gather strength and renew its purpose. To have an interesting or even learned essay read out to it will do not a bit of good. The community requires solid food, some basic iron rations, not flashy entertainment or scholarly acrobatics. For, the people of God at the Sunday Liturgy, gathered at ambo and altar as around the campfire at a staging post on the journey, longs to hear the stories of God's wonderful deeds among us, to be entranced and motivated and energized. For this we need real nourishment, not just a finger buffet.

Praying for the people of God

The prayers of the people are of course far too important a liturgical piece to be left to a clergy person, not even a deacon, and the chance should not be missed to engage lay members of the assembly in this ministry.

There are two stages in the development of shared ministry in the leading of the prayers of the people. First, the recruitment of many members of the assembly to provide different voices reading familiar prayers, either the set forms contained in our prayer books or in collections of prayers, or those composed 'in house' by local worship leaders. Second, the encouragement of lay members to take the further step of composing their own prayers based on the theme of the day, choosing a bidding and response, and leading the assembly.

The latter course is not without its risks, but a good set of guidelines from the pastor, together with a training session or two, will smooth out most wrinkles. Occasionally things may go awry, but even when they do, the great benefit for the whole assembly of prayers arising from the people for the people by far outweighs any falling away from that elusive state of liturgical perfection. This is real liturgy – the work of the people of God – with all the untidiness of a construction site.

Silence

When, in the final analysis, all words are found to be wanting, silence comes into its own. Silence should always be a component of a balanced and whole liturgy, for it corrects our tendency to reduce worship to an aimless chattering with God.

Silence within the liturgy is a thing of great beauty and prayerfulness, but must be treasured and defended against the nervous president and the agitated organist. For this reason it is essential to ensure that the silence appears intentional (as opposed to accidental silence occasioned by someone losing their place). Both the beginning and end of the period of silence should be announced by a clear signal.

A gong, such as those readily obtained from any Buddhist website, makes an excellent sound for this purpose. It must be kept firmly under the control of the president. Even the experienced president will feel an enormous pressure to keep the silence short; the nervous server stands no chance of mustering sufficient restraint to ensure an adequate silence.

Choreography

A typical Sunday Liturgy in Ordinary Time might take the pattern as follows:

- **At the chair:** the assembly, seated in a configuration expressive of community and participation, waits in silence. A few minutes before the service is due to start, the president and other liturgical ministers enter unobtrusively and take their seats. The president is vested in chasuble with the stole worn over it.

  Along with the rest of the assembly, the liturgical ministers wait in prayerful attentiveness for the liturgy to begin. This places the leadership firmly in the camp of fellow pilgrims along with everyone else, in this season of purposeful wandering and exploration. It signifies that we are in this together.

  At the appointed time, the ministers stand, and bow to the assembly. The president greets the people, announces the theme of the day and announces the song of journey to the font.

  Singing while we journey needs to be automatic, like humming a tune while we work. Clutching an order of service, trying not to lose your place, hoping you've got the right verse, are activities which detract from the job in hand: progressing joyfully and unselfconsciously from one part of the liturgical space to another.

  For this purpose, a hymn or song, no matter how well known, will not be the most appropriate musical vehicle. Instead, a repeated chant, a round, a refrain, should be used, or even a drum beat. Anything that doesn't require us to think too much yet lifts the mood of the assembly. The collection of chants and refrains called *Psallite* (2006) is a collaborative work of five composers and one example of an excellent resource which provides music on the theme of every Sunday of the three-year cycle.

- **At the font:** during the song, the assembly gathers around the font and remains standing. The president introduces the penitential rite, allowing time for silent reflection. After silence, the petitions of the penitential rite are said or sung, and following the absolution the assembly is sprinkled with water from the font. The president then invites the assembly to return to their places for the ministry of the Word.

- **At the ambo:** the assembly is seated on either side of the ambo, which is set in the midst of the nave, facing east. The president sings the prayer of the day, preferably using the appropriate collect from *Opening Prayers: Collects in Contemporary Language* (International Commission, 2001), which are prayers reflecting the gospel appointed for the day, and vastly superior to anything any of the denominations has yet come up with. The first reader then comes forward to receive the stole. President and reader bow to one another, the stole is placed around the reader's neck, and they bow once more. The assembly sits for the reading. After the reading the reader returns to the president, who removes the stole from the reader's neck. This procedure is repeated for the cantor of the psalm, the second reader, and for the deacon or other liturgical minister reading the Gospel. The gospeller goes to the altar table where the Gospel Book is enthroned, and processes with it to the ambo.

  The Gospel should first be announced – 'Hear the good news of our Lord Jesus Christ according to . . .' – and then censed. Time was when incense was a churchmanship issue occasioning lots of declarations of 'over my dead body'. Hopefully such controversy has for the most part petered out in an age when incense sticks and candles are sold in practically every craft shop from Lands End to John O'Groats. We need to grab with both hands any means of heightening the use of our senses in worship, and the use of incense (a scriptural feature if ever there was one) is liturgical shorthand for both sacrifice and the worship of the heavenly host.

  After the Gospel has been read, the Gospel Book is carried in procession round the assembly, so that the faithful may touch or kiss the book. The gospeller then returns to the president, who resumes wearing the stole if he/she is also the preacher. He/she preaches either seated at the chair, or standing at the ambo. If another is to preach, the preacher comes forward to receive the stole in the usual manner.

  After the homily, the president, again vested in the stole, sounds three times a gong or other instrument to signal the beginning of a period of silence. After a period of at least two minutes, the president sounds the gong once more, and invites the assembly to stand.

  The affirmation of faith follows, preferably using one of the many alternatives to the Nicene Creed provided in *Common Worship* (2000) (pp. 144–8), many of which are in responsorial form.

For the prayers of the people, the intercessor comes forward to receive the stole in the usual way, and leads the assembly in prayer, hopefully composed by him/herself rather than in a form out of a book. After the prayers, the intercessor returns the stole to the president.

The president then, beginning with an appropriate introductory sentence, announces the Peace. The deacon or other liturgical minister then invites the people to 'offer one another a sign of Christ's peace'. We share the peace of Christ at this point in obedience to Jesus' teaching that when we presume to bring gifts to the altar of God we must 'first be reconciled to your brother or sister' (Matthew 5.23). It is the position in the liturgy enjoined by Hippolytus, but passed over subsequently by the Roman Church in preference for a less significant moment just before communion. Just for once we Anglicans can bask in the more primitive use.

After a reasonably short time, the president draws the assembly back together by announcing the song of journey to the altar table. He/she explains the theological significance of what the assembly is about to do, and gives directions to those wishing to make an offering.

- **At the altar table:** approaching the altar table, members of the assembly carry in procession all that is necessary for the sacred meal, including the cloth, the fair linen, and the bread, wine and water.

  A basket for the financial offering should also be placed on the altar table, and the assembly invited to come forward to place their contributions there. This approach is far more user-friendly than having a plate thrust under one's nose (with or without menace) and is symbolic of a more wholesome theology of the household of God in which guests are not expected to pay for the hospitality we offer them.

  It is important that the offering basket remain on the altar table throughout the eucharistic prayer. In this we affirm that the offering of money is today's version of the offering of the fruits of the earth, and acceptable to God, not something to be hurriedly taken from the altar table after the offertory, as if sordid or unworthy.

  The assembly encircles the altar table, the president standing as part of the circle, at the same distance from the table as everyone else. The president censes the gifts of bread and wine and the offering. The president then bows to the assembly and censes the people slowly and solemnly. This is no task to be delegated to a minion, for in censing the assembly, the servant of the servants of God is reminding them that they are holy, and set apart, holier even than the gifts provided in God's abundance for their spiritual food.

  The president then invites the people to offer themselves to God as a priestly people, as a suitable song of offering is sung. A good example is 'Take, O take me

Incense in the Liturgy

Traditional Catholic ritual made a great play of censing the altar and the gifts at this point, while delegating to a server a last-minute and rather perfunctory censing of the congregation. This way of doing things actually reverses the logical, and indeed scriptural, order of things. Jesus pointed out to the religious establishment of his day that in ritual matters they tended to make a great fuss about subsidiary matters while ignoring the source. 'How blind you are! For which is greater, the gift or the altar that makes the gift sacred?' (Matthew 23.19).

To extend that thought a little further, and to get to the heart of the matter as Jesus intended, we should ask ourselves which is the greater: the gifts and the altar on which they lie, or the community that offers and consecrates them?

The censing of the assembly, the holy priestly community of faith, should therefore be more significant than the censing of the gifts and the altar. Where the assembly is gathered around the altar table the president should make quite a thing of coming to the centre, bowing to the community, and then censing everyone in a slow and stately manner by going round the whole circle, then bowing once again upon completion.

Furthermore, there is much to be said for reversing the customary order: first censing the people who have gathered to make the offering, and then the gifts we offer for God's blessing and the altar table in our midst on which we do the offering. That would help establish a theological pecking order that makes sense.

Of course for many parishes all this talk of censing may seem academic, given the innate resistance to incense in some quarters, and the prevalence of congregants who, panic stricken, will stuff handkerchiefs in their mouths whenever a thurible passes within a hundred metres of them. Like candles, icons and prayer mats, however, incense has now passed into general circulation as the currency of those seeking a spiritual dimension to their lives. For the Church to get hung up on whether any such item is 'Catholic' or 'Evangelical', 'High' or 'Low', would be to expose our total lack of connection to what is going on in the real world.

The use of incense in Judaeo-Christian ritual is threaded through our Scriptures from beginning to end. From the children of Israel on their wilderness journey, to the angel of incense in the Book of Revelation, incense has been our shorthand for sacrificial worship and a symbol of the prayers of the saints rising to God's presence, and the psalmist exclaimed: 'Let my prayer be counted as incense before you' (Psalm 141.2). It is therefore odd indeed of us now to come over all prim and prissy about the stuff of heaven. Far better to break ourselves in right now with a little gentle practise in the incense department, especially on grand occasions, so that the scent of the heavenly places may sweeten the offering of our assemblies. If thurible-swinging is a little too much, a suitable bowl (i.e. not one that will crack with the heat) should be placed on the floor or on a stand in the midst of the assembly before the altar table, in which incense is burned.

as I am' from the Iona Community, which makes a powerful act of self offering of the assembly once gathered around the altar table. It consists only of four lines, easily learnt, and can be repeated several times and hummed the final time. Simple actions go with it, and corny as it may sound, the simple effectiveness of this song at this moment in the liturgy reduces many a seasoned veteran to tears.

Song of Offering

'Take, O take me, as I am'[1]

Take O take me as I am	– *hands extended before one*
Summon out what I shall be	– *hands extended and raised*
Set your seal upon my heart	– *right hand on forehead, mouth and heart*
And live in me	– *hands extended, brought together above the head in a circular motion, and brought down in front of one, held together.*

For the eucharistic prayer the president stands where he/she can see and be seen, and the side of the altar table he/she chooses will no doubt vary from season to season. In Advent, as we shall see, the president may stand on the west side looking east, embodying expectation and longing for that which lies beyond us. More often, the natural position will tend to be on the east side looking west, in a spirit of engagement with a waiting world.

Whatever the season, the president stands well back from the table. Though directing and co-ordinating this liturgical action, the president remains at all times a member of the assembly, and should take up a position in the gathering that articulates that. This sounds the death knell for manual acts exclusive to the president. Instead, what manual acts there are become the common property of the assembly, shared by all.

The whole assembly therefore acts as a single body instead of as a group of individuals observing a rite.

The president invites the whole assembly to place their orders of service on the floor and to raise their hands, with him/her, in the *orans* posture of prayer as the eucharistic prayer, recited by the president alone, is offered by the whole people of God. To signify this common consecration, the president remains as part of the circle, standing back from the altar, and refrains from manual acts. The prayer culminates in the singing of the Sanctus.

A further step may be taken by the adventurous president to ensure that every member of the assembly adds their voice to the eucharistic prayer. The assembly can be invited to sing softly a repeated 'Alleluia' to notes provided by the musician, which is maintained *sostenuto* throughout the eucharistic prayer while the president chants the prayer over it. If the president does not feel confident enough to sing this ad lib, the prayer could be spoken over the chanted Alleluia.

The president then invites the people to make a profound bow of reverence before the mystery of God's presence. In this way the whole assembly, acting as one, models the theological insight that the priesthood being exercised here is not the prerogative of a sacerdotal caste but the common possession and shared task of the holy people of God.

The president then invites the members of the assembly to join hands and say the Lord's Prayer.

The president moves forward to the altar table, bows deeply, and breaks the bread. The Agnus Dei or other fraction anthem then follows, while the bread is broken and distributed to the patens, and the wine is poured into four cups which are then placed at each corner of the altar table.

The president and another liturgical minister then hold up a paten and cup while first explaining the method of communion and then inviting all present to take part. The liturgical ministers first administer the holy bread to the people standing where they are in the circle, and then the members of the assembly come forward to the altar table to take a cup into their own hands and drink from it (not dip bread into it). Anyone not wishing to share the common cup is asked to receive Holy Communion in one kind only.

When all have received, the president invites the people again to make a deep bow, and then return to their places around the ambo.

- **At the ambo:** the president again sounds the gong three times to signal a period of silence, after which it is sounded once. The reflection song follows, the assembly seated.

The president then invites the assembly to rise, and says the post-communion prayer. The assembly is then invited to sit for the announcements, given by a warden or other lay leader of the community.

The president then calls forward any member of the community who has asked for a blessing, or who is to be commissioned to a new ministry, or sent forth on a new beginning.

The president then pronounces the blessing, if there is one, and the deacon or other liturgical minister gives the sending out.

The president and other ministers then make their way to the exit, there to greet the people, while an organ voluntary or other music is played.

See-at-a-glance Liturgy in Ordinary Time

Chair

Entrance – ministers emerge from the community
Greeting
Song of journey

Font

Penitential rite
Sprinkling
Song of journey

Ambo

Prayer of the day
Reading from Hebrew Scriptures
Psalm
Reading from Christian Scriptures
Alleluia
Gospel
Procession of Gospel Book
Homily

Silence

Affirmation of faith
Prayers of the people

The Peace
Song of journey

Altar table

Song of offering
The eucharistic prayer
Sanctus
Lord's Prayer
Breaking of the bread
Communion
Invitation to reflection

Ambo

Silence

Song of reflection
Post-communion prayer
Announcements
Sending out

Music in Ordinary Time

A sample of music from different sources to enrich a typical Sunday Liturgy in Ordinary Time. See Appendix 3 for full publishing details.

Song of journey (to the font)

'Come rejoice before our maker', Noel Tredinnick, in *The Complete Celebration Hymnal*.

Penitential rite

'Kyries', Richard Shepherd, in *The Addington Service*.

Sprinkling song

'O Blessed Spring', Robert Buckley Farlee, in *Wonder, Love and Praise*.

Psalm

'Shepherd me, O God' (Psalm 23), in *Singing the Psalms* and *Gather*.

Gospel acclamation

'Alleluia', Richard Proulx, in *Gather*.

Song of journey (to the altar table)

'As new born stars were stirred to song', John Karl Hirten, in *Wonder, Love and Praise*.

Song of offering

'Take, O take me as I am', John Bell, in *Come All You People*.

Communion

'What do you want of me, Lord?', Donna Marie McGargill OSM, in *Breaking Bread Hymnal*.

Song of reflection

'O God you search me and you know me', Bernadette Farrell, in *Breaking Bread Hymnal* and *Glory and Praise*.

Notes

1 From John L. Bell, *Come All You People*, GIA Publications, 1994.

2 ADVENT

Advent, the season leading up to Christmas, is probably everybody's favourite. The goose is getting fat, chestnuts will soon be roasting by an open fire, and returning home as dusk falls makes one think of toast and marmite round the kitchen range.

Advent: the liturgical ministers facing east

Historical background

The first clear references to Advent appear in the sixth century, and by the eighth century special collects, epistles and gospels had been provided (in the Gelasian Sacramentary) for the five Sundays preceding Christmas as well as for the intervening Wednesdays and Fridays. This indicates that Advent was originally seen as a penitential season similar to Lent. But the Western Church evidently has a limited capacity for fasting, the five Sundays soon being reduced to four,[1] and the penance toned down. In the Eastern Church, however, Advent is a much longer season beginning in the middle of November, an approach which the Church of England attempted to revive with its 'Nine Sundays before Christmas' of the *Alternative Service Book 1980*, with little success.

Characteristics

The word Advent comes from the Latin *adventus* (coming), and is meant to refocus our attention, at the end of a long series of Sundays in Ordinary Time, on the coming of Christ. The season conceals something of a tug of war between the Church's intention and human inclination. Although Advent is concerned with the coming of Christ in both historical and eschatalogical terms, the original emphasis on the end time, and the coming of Christ in glory 'to judge the living and the dead' (Nicene Creed), has tended with the passing of the centuries to be overshadowed by the countdown to the birth of Christ.

Advent can be termed 'penitential lite'. It retains some marks of a penitential season, such as purple vestments (though even this is relaxed in softie circles for the Third Sunday '*Gaudate*'), and the omission of the Gloria in the eucharist. None of this need keep us awake at night. Although festivities are discouraged (a good excuse for clergy to avoid weddings), and flowers frowned upon, fasting is no longer ordered or expected in the Western Church.

Cultural context

Today we find ourselves amidst an emasculated Advent, a season conveniently tamed by our culture into a mere preface to the celebrations around the birth of Jesus. In every home the Advent calendar disgorges its mini bars of chocolate as we edge nearer C Day, and in every church the ubiquitous Advent wreath is equally effective in restricting this season to manageable non-threatening proportions.

I can still remember hearing, as an impressionable teenager, sermons (one particularly scary one at St Aidan's, Small Heath) warning of the awful sudden Judgement that was to fall upon us in the Second Coming. A cataclysmic event of which Advent was a sobering reminder. It seems however that the days when such a message could carry weight in mainstream Christianity are effectively over. For better or for worse the grip of the contemporary Church on the doctrine of the Second Coming gets looser by the minute, and it is no bad thing. Other emphases are necessary to excite the human heart at the story of Jesus the Christ and to elicit an active response leading to transformation. Further talk of the thief in the night is probably not going to do it.

Even when it comes to the observance of Advent as a penitential period with the more limited scope of preparing for the commemoration of Jesus' birth, the Christian Church finds itself spitting in the wind when it comes to making a go of it in the context of the Western culture of instant gratification. When the shopping mall is blasting out carols from mid autumn, the pastor who attempts to stem the tide of carols in worship until Christmas Eve begins to feel more and more like King Canute trying to stem the ocean waves (and he had only the ripples of the Wash to contend with).

What should be done? Advent presents the Christian community with a fork-in-the-road decision about its role in society. Does it go with the flow, or offer a counter-cultural experience? To go with the cultural flow would mean extending Advent to correlate to the pre-Christmas shopping season, and thereby make it even more diffuse and meaningless. If the Church means to have anything to say, it seems that we have little choice but to offer something different: a reflective period of stillness, seeking and preparation amidst the craziness.

We may trim the sails here and there (an Advent carol service can cover a few if not a multitude of liturgical sins), but the attempt will have been made and the point will remain. Any attempt to make sense of the season of Advent will be deeply valued by all who seek respite from the headlong dash of the lemmings into disillusion and debt.

Planning and preparation

As we approach any of the special festivals or seasons of the Church's Year, it is highly desirable to make the planning and preparation as far as possible a communal enterprise. This heightens awareness of our movement through the seasons, and increases the sense of ownership in all that we offer God in worship.

The excellent workbook *Crafts for Creative Worship* by Jan Brind and Tessa Wilkinson (2004) is a rich resource for faith communities wishing to start again, doing it properly this time. The authors advocate a good chunk of a Saturday one week before the next season begins should be given over to communal preparation, which will include preparing materials with which to decorate the worship space, making teaching or liturgical aids, learning new music, rehearsing a play, and cooking. It should be an all-age fun activity and include a meal together.

Choreography

Advent: the configuration of the liturgical space

Setting

Advent is both a penitential season and a time of expectant journey, of waiting upon God. John the Baptizer is a central figure, so this is no time for frivolity. As the Church seeks to 'prepare the way of the Lord' (Mark 1.3), the liturgical room is kept plain and simple. There should be no flowers or greenery, but sometimes an arrangement of bare branches can be effective as a reminder of the wilderness experience.

The font or baptismal pool should be drained during Advent, as a powerful sign of our thirsting for God. An explanatory sign should be positioned near the font so the point is not missed. This may read:

ADVENT
The season of Advent
(the four Sundays before Christmas)
is a time of preparation, prayer and fasting.
It is a wilderness time,
dominated by the
figure of
John the Baptizer
who announced the
coming of the Holy One,
and who called upon
God's people to repent.
For this reason the font is
drained during Advent,
to recall us to our thirsting for God.

Purple (preferably reddish purple) is the liturgical colour for Advent, and in keeping with the season this should be understated. Vestments should speak through colour alone, not through busy patterned or decorated surfaces. The habit of draping swaths of purple cloth here, there and everywhere (over the drained font for example) should be resisted.

Orientation

Advent may retain only the last vestiges of a penitential season, but coming where it does in relation to Christmas (culturally as well as religiously understood) it demands of the Church an intentional reorientation over against prevailing norms.

Advent: the assembly at the altar table faces east

The most significant way in which such a stance can be expressed is in the arrangement of the physical space in which the assembly will gather for the four Sundays of Advent. It needs to look quite different. A change of basic orientation will impact more forcefully on the consciousness of the worshipper than any amount of sermons or explanatory pamphlets.

Remember, no church building exists which cannot be satisfactorily reconfigured, given the desire and the political will to do so. As we look again at the Church's Year with a view to enlivening our liturgical expression of each season, fast or feast, an inflexible worship space will become more and more an unacceptable obstacle to everything we are trying to say and do and become.

The supreme advantage of worship spaces with a high degree of flexibility is their capacity for ringing the changes through the Church's Year, giving to each season a distinct seating plan which helps make explicit the liturgical emphasis of that season.

In penitential seasons it is appropriate to express the *metanoia* (turning around) of repentance by turning around the furniture to enable the assembly to face in another direction.

Peter Doll (2005), in his booklet *Liturgy and Architecture for a Pilgrim People*, reminds us of the pitfalls inherent in a liturgical seating plan which is unvaryingly turned in upon itself. Following centuries of hierarchical seating plans which compartmentalized worship space between players and spectators, the liturgical reforms which sprang from Vatican II and which reunited the assembly as a priestly community gathered around centralized liturgical foci were a desperately needed corrective.

Doll recalls us to the view, however, that for a balanced liturgical diet we need to supplement looking inwards with periods when we look beyond; away from ourselves to that which is totally other. Immanence needs to be balanced by transcendence.

Doll argues that, from earliest times, 'there is no evidence that the priest's facing the people in the celebration was ever a priority in itself. Rather the priority was always celebration towards the east' (Doll, 2005, p. 19). Turning towards the east is 'a sign of the Church's anticipation of and participation in Christ's final coming in glory, his rising in the East as the sun of righteousness'.

Doll's vision of president and people turning east in prayer as they 'go in pilgrimage together towards the consummation of all things' (p. 19) is, however, a very far cry indeed from the priest's mutter into the wall at that weekly festival of individualism called the 8 o'clock Communion. It is all too easy for scholarly notions about pilgrim people to be hijacked by neo-conservatives looking to justify a headlong flight from liturgical renewal.

Michael Lang (2004), in *Turning Towards the Lord*, argues for the priority, both theologically and historically, of the eastward-facing position for the whole assembly, priest included. Indeed, he maintains that the practical liturgical instructions emanating from Vatican II permit and recommend the relocation of the altar away from the east wall, but do not proscribe it. Likewise, claims Lang, the position at the altar taken by the priest: celebrating *versus populum* is encouraged but not made compulsory. However skillfully Lang may peel back the nuances of the original Latin texts, he fails to do justice to the tidal wave of reform that overran all liturgical churches in the latter decades of the twentieth century, following centuries of rigid conformity.

When Lang speaks of a whole assembly facing east, he can make it sound good: 'the Mass is a common act of worship where priest and people together, representing the pilgrim Church, reach out for the transcendent God' (Lang, 2004, p. 32). Here he sounds plausible as a fellow explorer seeking to further interpret the insights of Vatican II, but in reality such ideas can be used as a Trojan horse to slip into the camp and turn all our clocks back while we sleep. The vision articulated by Lang is unrecognizable when we stumble in upon a gaggle of individuals scattered across an empty nave, doing their level best to avoid any contact with their fellow Christians and (with a bit of luck) God too, or upon a Tridentine Latin mass celebrated triumphantly, not by pilgrims, but by those who know they have arrived.

Lang may have his work cut out to convince us that such hole-in-the-corner liturgies are exercises in transcendent spirituality, but nevertheless he has a point, provided his position is seen as an occasional useful corrective rather than a whole-sale alternative.

Advent is a particularly appropriate season for reintroducing a sense of looking beyond our own little circle of liturgical wagons. During Advent the assembly can be invited to turn and look east during the penitential rite, the prayer for the day and the prayers of the people. They may also be invited to raise their hands during times of prayer in the *orans* posture of supplication and praise.

Such a change in direction is particularly effective when the assembly is normally seated in choir formation or in a semi-circle or on three sides of a square. Even when seated in eastward-facing fixed seating, however, at least a glimpse of this change in orientation can be achieved if the leaders of worship, instead of leading prayer facing the people, turn to pray facing east. Leaders should avoid praying with their backs to the people, but instead move to a position in the midst of the assembly to pray facing east from there.

'East' in this situation is not necessarily the compass point, but is what makes liturgical sense. If for example the liturgical space is dominated by a window or a work of art redolent of the transcendence and majesty of God, or if the structure of the building itself summons the eye in a certain direction, that will do just fine. The point is to allow into our assembly the dimension of that which is beyond us and not in our control. To achieve this, whatever works will suffice.

Presidency

The reorientation of the assembly is further emphasized by the positioning of the president's chair, with those who preside beginning the leadership of the liturgy from a different place than is customary at other times. In Advent the president's chair can be placed at the west end of the liturgical space, facing east, which is in itself a powerful symbol of a whole different approach. Alternatively, the president may remain at the chair in the customary position to address the assembly, but move to stand in the midst of the assembly facing east, to address God in prayer and to call on God on behalf of the people in the penitential rite. This also can make a dramatic impact.

Liturgical furniture

The positioning of the liturgical foci of ambo and altar table will need to be determined by what works best for providing the assembly with an experience of turning to face a new direction.

In addition, a further visual focus may be required, especially in situations where we symbolically look beyond the body of the assembly to that which is beyond. What exactly do we look at?

Where we have antiphonal seating on either side of a central liturgical axis, with the president leading worship by standing among the people looking east, we face an empty slot where we are accustomed to some form of visual focus. This can either be left empty, the vacancy used to explain that we deliberately maintain a gap in the circle to signify the absent but coming Lord, or alternatively we might insert a seasonal focus.

One helpful option is to place at the east end of the space the Book of the Gospels on a stand draped with purple cloth. This signifies the presence of Christ in his words presiding over the assembly, and can be incorporated in the liturgical action if the gospeller carries the Book of the Gospels in solemn procession to the ambo from the stand for the proclamation, and then returns it there, to remain 'enthroned' through-out the rest of the liturgy.

The Sunday Liturgy

For the season of Advent, the Sunday Liturgy might incorporate the following seasonal features:

Entrance

Advent is a good time to begin the Sunday Liturgy in a new and startling way which will wake us from liturgical stupor. One option is to darken the space (turning down the lights usually suffices) and to have declaimed by a disembodied voice (a reader standing in a gallery or transept) a short passage from one of the Hebrew prophets enshrining a suitable wake-up call. Sections from the prophecy of Isaiah are particu-larly appropriate, such as 1.1–7, beginning:

> *Hear, O heavens, and listen, o earth; for the Lord has spoken:*
> *I reared children and brought them up,*
> *But they have rebelled against me.*

or 5.8–13, beginning:

> *Ah, you who join house to house, who add field to field, until there is room for no one but you.*

or 6.9–12, beginning:

> *And he said, 'Go and say to this people:*
> *Keep listening, but do not comprehend,*
> *Keep looking, but do not understand.'*

A strong voice, not over-dramatic but forceful, declaiming such passages, as it were out of nowhere, in a dimly lit worship space, can certainly produce a tingle factor and get things off to a flying Advent start.

Another is to play over the sound system, or have sung for us if our musicians are up to it, the opening song from *Godspell*, 'Prepare ye the way of the Lord', or some such piece of popular music with a similar theme, to prod us out of slumber.

As the lights come up, the ministers enter during the singing of the Advent Prose and take their positions at the chair at the west end of the liturgical space, facing east, with the assembly on either side and the ambo in front of them, also facing east. The Advent Prose (thirteenth century) makes an ideal litany of entrance, or alternatively can be incorporated as part of the penitential rite. Either way, it should be used every Sunday in Advent come what may. It is simply too hauntingly beautiful to be missed.[2]

Penitential rite

After greeting the people, the president invites the assembly to turn east as a sign of waiting and of looking to our furthest horizon for the God who is among us but who is yet to come. The president then introduces the penitential rite in the context of the Advent theme of preparing the way of the Lord, the assembly still facing east. The Advent Prose can be sung here as a prayer of penitence, if not already used as an entrance litany, and the general absolution follows.

Lighting the Advent wreath

The consecutive lighting of four candles during Advent, one for each Sunday, has now become in many congregations the central ritual act of the season. Originally of Scandinavian, presumably Lutheran, provenance, this custom has leapt all ecumenical boundary walls and is now ensconced as an inviolable custom not to be meddled with lightly.

It is harmless enough, but should be kept in check. The Advent wreath is of course grabbed hold of as an ideal moment in which to involve children, but it further consolidates the culture's countdown to Christmas and firmly directs attention away from the embarrassing notion of the last things.

The Advent wreath installation should be designed in proportion to the liturgical space and to its peripheral importance in the liturgy. It should dominate neither the space nor the liturgy. A good place to insert it is after the penitential rite and before the ministry of the Word, indicating that it takes place only after the serious business of making our peace with God, and is not part of the Liturgy of the Word proper. It should also be made as simple as possible. Four white candles is all anyone needs, unless one is an ecclesiastical supplies merchant anxious to create demand where there is no need. A different colour for the Third Sunday in so short a season seems plainly ridiculous.

The prayer of the day

The president again invites the assembly to turn to face east, and intones the prayer of the day. The Liturgy of the Word follows in the normal way.

The Gospel

The deacon or person appointed to read the Gospel goes to the stand at the east end of the liturgical space where the Book of the Gospels is enthroned, and carries it in solemn procession through the midst of the assembly to the ambo. After the Gospel, the Book of the Gospels is returned to the stand at the east end, but is carried through the assembly slowly, in such a way that members of the assembly are given an opportunity to reach out and touch the Gospel Book as worshippers do in the synagogue when the scroll of the Torah is carried through their midst.

The affirmation of faith

The way in which we affirm our faith provides another good opportunity to mark and distinguish between the seasons. In addition to the customary Nicene Creed there are many alternatives available to sharpen our awareness of what we are about, and avoid the comatose repetition of over familiar texts. If in doubt, a suitable passage from the New Testament should be sufficiently reassuring and incontrovertible to all but the most fanatical of purists.

The eucharistic prayer

Following the sharing of the Peace, the president invites the assembly to move with him/her to gather round the altar table, there to offer together the priestly prayer of the whole community. Whereas usually the president would stand at the east side of the altar table with the community forming a circle around it, in Advent the president stands on the west side facing east. The community stands on either side of him/her in a horseshoe formation with the open end towards the east.

The Book of the Gospel on its stand remains visible as a visual focus in the gap, but the opening remains a powerful symbol of the incomplete and provisional nature of all that we do as we carry out the work of the people of God in performing the liturgy. As Richard Meux Benson, founder of the Cowley Fathers, always taught, we should celebrate the eucharist in the expectation of the glory of God breaking through at any moment.

Communion

The way in which we share communion is also something that can change with the seasons (see *Creating Uncommon Worship* (Giles, 2004a) for more extensive treatment of this subject).

In some seasons the consecrated bread may be administered by the leaders, or passed member to member through the assembly, while the chalices are placed on the corners of the altar table where the faithful approach the table and themselves take the cup into their own hands. At other times the bread may be passed around the assembly in baskets until each member holds a piece, and then is consumed simultaneously.

These are but two of the many options available in sharing the sacrament among members of the assembly, but a common feature when the community is already gathered around the altar table for the eucharistic prayer is that there will be a natural emphasis on sharing one with another rather than on having the sacrament administered to us. The niceties of who is and who is not authorized to minister the sacrament are rendered superfluous as we rediscover the simple theological insight that all members of the Christian community without exception are so authorized by their baptism.

Post communion

While the purists point, quite correctly, to the direct line between communion and commissioning for service in the world, the more fragile among us need a moment's reflection on what we have received and what we have become, before taking on the restructuring of society. After communion we should therefore pause for a time of silence, with music that feeds this reflective mood. This will usually be done by returning from the altar table to take our seats round the ambo again, but in Advent it is good to ring the changes.

This can be done by the president inviting the assembly after communion to disperse through the liturgical space and find a corner where they can be still. The lights are dimmed, and after a suitable period of silence, perhaps just two minutes, some suitable music is sung by the few for the many, or a poem or meditation is read. Resources for such brief meditations are numerous, but among the most helpful are the Iona Community's seasonal material, for example *Cloth for the Cradle: Worship Resources and Readings for Advent, Christmas and Epiphany* (Wild Goose Resource Group, 2000).

At the conclusion of this interlude the lights are brought back and everyone returns to their seats for the post-communion prayer, announcements and dismissal.

See-at-a-glance Liturgy in Advent

Chair

Advent acclamation
Entrance – the Advent Prose sung in procession
Greeting
Penitential rite
Lighting the Advent wreath

Ambo

Prayer of the day
Reading from the Hebrew Scriptures
Psalm
Reading from the Christian Scriptures
Gospel acclamation
Gospel

Procession of Gospel Book
Homily

Silence

Affirmation of faith
Prayers of the people

The Peace
Song of journey

Altar table

Song of offering
The eucharistic prayer
Sanctus
Lord's Prayer
Breaking of the bread
Communion
Reflection (dispersed)

Ambo

Post-communion prayer
Announcements
Sending out

Music in Advent

A typical selection of music for the Sunday Liturgy in Advent. See Appendix 3 for full publishing details.

Wake-up call

'People look East', Besançon Carol, in *Breaking Bread Hymnal* and *Advent for Choirs*.

Entrance process

Advent Prose (English), Stephen Cleobury, in *Advent for Choirs*.

Lighting the Advent wreath

'Blessed are you, sovereign Lord', Malcolm Archer, in *Advent for Choirs*.

Psalm

'To you, O Lord' (Psalm 25), Bob Hurd, in *Singing the Psalms*.

Gospel acclamation

'Praise to you, O Christ our Saviour', Bernadette Farrell, *Glory and Praise* and *The Complete Celebration Hymnal*.

Song of journey (to the altar table)

'In the Day of the Lord', M. D. Ridge, in *Breaking Bread Hymnal* and OCP Publications (sheet music).

Song of offering

'I wait for the Lord', Alan Shellard, in *Cantate*.

Communion

'O come, O come, Emmanuel', plainsong mode 1.

Final song

'Jerusalem my happy home' (tune: 'Land of Rest'), in *The Hymnal 1982*.

Not a Carol Service: a non-liturgical service for Advent

Invitations to 'Not a Carol Service' are distributed widely throughout our neighbourhood. The invitation has all the trappings of a Carol Service (a sprig of holly in the corner etc.) while clearly stating what it is not.

Opening hymn: 'O Come all ye faithful'

Opening sentence and welcome

Second hymn: 'While shepherds watched'

During this hymn, the service is interrupted by a member of the faith community acting the part of an amiable drunk who engages the worship leader in an exchange about the meaning of what's going on.

The drunk ushers in his heavily pregnant girlfriend. They have nowhere to sleep that night; consternation, embarrassment.

Not knowing what to do, the organist strikes up 'Away in a manger' and the congregation manages a few lines before the drunk interrupts again, demanding attention and help.

The worship leader invites the young couple to come up and sit beside him / her, and suggests the assembly listen to a story.

Reading: Luke 10.29–37, The Parable of the Good Samaritan

Homily

Song: 'Bread for the World', Bernadette Farrell (OCP Publications)

Witness: Stories by two or three members of the faith community about their church's life and work.

Song: 'What do you want of me Lord?', Donna Marie Cargill OSM (*Breaking Bread Hymnal*)

Prayers

Hymn: 'O Come, O Come, Emmanuel'

Blessing

Refreshments served afterwards at which the faith community is focused and organized in its welcome of visitors and newcomers.

Notes

1 In years when Advent 4 coincides with Christmas Eve (as in 2006) it is not unknown for parishes (especially of the Roman obedience it seems) to dispense with Advent 4 altogether. And then there were three . . .

2 *Advent for Choirs*, Oxford University Press, 2000

3 CHRISTMAS

Christmas: the liturgical space prepared

The feast of Christmas celebrates the birth of Jesus the Christ. What originally grew out of the natural curiosity of devoted followers about the place and date of the birth of their Lord and Saviour subsequently developed into an affirmation of the doctrine of the incarnation, the entry of the divine and eternal Son of God into human life. Associated with this came an increasing devotion to Mary, mother of the Lord, who with time was hailed as no less than *theotokos*, God-bearer.

Historical background

Given the primitive recording procedures current at the time, there is of course no way the Church could ever have determined the actual date of Christ's birth. Instead they went one better, and came up with a public relations coup which one liturgical scholar has described as 'sheer pastoral genius' (R. F. Buxton in Davies (ed.), 1986).

The date of 25 December was purely speculative, and had more to do with the winter solstice than with any inside information as to when this special birth actually took place. The golden opportunity for a takeover came in 274 CE when the Emperor Aurelian, little suspecting what a wily lot the Christians were, had the temerity to inaugurate a festival in honour of the Invincible Sun, *Natalis Solis Invicti*. The Church simply took this over as the feast of the Son, an audacious masterstroke, which combined the human need for a party around the shortest day of the year with delight in the birth of a child, especially one hailed as God-with-us.

This Christianization of pagan festivals and institutions became a trademark of an upbeat young Church which, despite undergoing occasional periods of brutal suppression, brimmed with confidence at its own destiny. This is perhaps difficult to conceive in an age like ours where secularism has the upper hand, but the facts speak for themselves. 'The bigger they come the harder they fall' seems to have been the Church's motto during the early centuries, and sure enough, the Roman Empire itself became, unbelievably, the Church's biggest catch, albeit in a way which was to leave the victor compromised and enfeebled for evermore.

Others of a more prosaic frame of mind determined the birth date by simply counting nine months from 25 March, the alleged date of the annunciation of Jesus' birth by the angel Gabriel to Mary. Hippolytus and Tertullian also understood 25 March as the date of the crucifixion, so 25 December has a kind of neatness to it.

At any rate, whatever theory is preferred, it took the Church nearly four hundred years to nail it down. The earliest evidence for the date is found in 336 CE (in the Philocalian Calendar describing contemporary Roman practice). With the conversion of the Emperor Constantine in 312, the date of 25 December to mark Christ's birthday gained currency and spread rapidly from Rome. In the Church of the East, however, the process took a little longer, given the primacy of the baptism of Christ. In the Armenian Church to this day, 6 January is the only day specifically devoted to the incarnation.

The theological controversies of the fourth to sixth centuries concerning the Person of Christ contributed to greater emphasis on 25 December as the Feast of the Incarnation, and to its politicization as a useful stick with which to bash heretics. Over the last century or so there has been a significant decline in the importance attached to Christmas, now generally regarded as being of secondary importance to Easter.

After all, birth narratives occur in only two of the four Gospels, and over the last hundred years New Testament scholarship has led to widespread questioning of their historical authenticity.

Characteristics

Christmas in liturgical terms is strictly speaking a dual celebration, of both the birth of Jesus, reputedly at Bethlehem though just as probably at Nazareth, and of the incarnation of the cosmic Christ, a mystery that can be approached only by poetic metaphor.

Whichever theme is uppermost, the feast calls for liturgical partying of the first order. Vestments are white, and the liturgical space is decorated to the nines with every conceivable trimming.

The dual character of the feast is reflected in the very different ethos of worship of the first mass of Christmas celebrated the evening before compared with that of Christmas morning. The eve of Christmas, much frequented by cultural Christians, tends to be a nostalgic candle-lit affair in which the blessing of the crib containing figures of Mary and Joseph with the Christ Child plays a key part. The gospel reading at the eucharist is always from the birth narratives contained in the Gospels of Matthew and Luke.

On Christmas morning, however, the mood is quite different. The readings are from the prologue of John's Gospel in praise of the eternal Word, and from the Letter to the Hebrews. The emphasis shifts to a theological meditation on the eternal significance of the birth of Christ recognized as 'the reflection of God's glory and the exact imprint of God's very being' (Hebrews 1.3).

Contemporary context

Christmas is a confusing occasion in relation to contemporary culture, leaving the Church never quite sure whether it presents a challenge or an opportunity. The primitive need to defy the darkest period of winter with merrymaking is common to all societies, especially in northern Europe, and was given a huge boost in the nineteenth century by the Prince Consort's imported Christmas tree and by the works of Charles Dickens.

The Church's Christianization of pagan festivals in the first centuries, while a master stroke of cultural colonization, also leaves the Church with many problems today. Christmas thrives as a major cultural and commercial festival even when stripped of religious meaning, and has to be reclaimed and in some respects re-invented by the Church if it is to retain any spiritual significance.

With regard to the dual liturgical character of the feast, the relative importance of worship the evening before or the morning after will largely depend on local circum-stances and the make-up of the regular congregation. Midnight Mass exactly at 12 a.m. is now something of a rarity, and the celebration of the birth of Jesus now tends to take place at any time during the previous evening to suit local circumstances.

The morning celebration on Christmas Day may in some places be almost extinct while in others (for example where young families with children predominate) it may take precedence over the night before.

Choreography

Proclamation

Because Christmas still presents the Church with a major evangelistic opportunity, it is helpful where possible to make a difference to the outside as well as the inside of the church building.

Setting

One reason why the liturgical space should remain very plain and understated during Advent is to provide a marked contrast to the sudden transformation of the church interior on Christmas Eve. The transformation should be dramatic, and is best carried out, not by a secret society of the specially chosen who have always retained control, but by the whole congregation. A time should be chosen by the leadership when the maximum number of people of all ages can gather to enter into the fun of transforming the liturgical space for the birthday celebration.

For maximum participation a good time may be following the eucharist of Advent 4 when a simple bread and soup lunch can be served and the whole community invited to lend a hand. It is worth involving (even if we have to offer them an hon-orarium) one or two animateurs of this kind of thing who can mobilize a diverse group of people to make decorations, arrange greenery and flowers, or build a crib. Such an event may mean that we have to sacrifice the liturgical purity of one or two weekdays of Advent, but, if so, this is a case when the nurture of our communal life trumps liturgical correctness.

Orientation

For Christmas the liturgical space will most probably be returned to its regular configuration, on the grounds that special arrangements should be kept for those periods (such as penitential seasons) when we are deliberately moving out of what is comfortable and reassuring. For party time we are majoring on relaxation, so will naturally gravitate to the layout that is familiar rather than challenging.

Presidency

On a major feast like Christmas, there is no need for the president to be a shrinking violet. Rather, it is one occasion when the president's confident, though not flamboyant, leadership will help 'lift' the liturgy and help give it a special character. The president's chair should be placed wherever it makes sense visually for a large gathering on a major feast.

Liturgical furniture

For Christmas, the liturgical foci will be placed in their normal positions appropriate for those occasions when the faith community is 'at home' to the wider community and showing its liturgical space to best advantage. Where possible, the seating of the assembly should always reflect the faith community's self-understanding of its character and role, that is, if it sees itself as a fully participatory community of ministries, then the seating configuration must be antiphonal, or in the round, or occupy three sides of a square. The exact configuration does not matter, provided that traditional seating in rows facing one direction, indicative of a passive audience watching a show, is avoided. Such a seating plan would simply not do justice to what the community is.

Eucharistic liturgy: Christmas Eve

Exterior

Given the residual affection among the general population for Christmas and for some degree of religious observance attached to it, we should help the church building put on its best bib and tucker for the passers by.

Presenting the church building in the best possible light, together with effective signposting, is one way to get off to a good start in attracting a crowd. A cheap but effective way of doing this is to line the approach path with lit candles set in paper bags weighted with sand. It sounds implausible but it actually works, as can be seen in parishes across North America. Strange to relate, the paper bags do their job as wind shields better than one would ever imagine, and they do not catch fire. The visual impact of dozens of candles leading the passer-by to the church door is extremely effective.

Entrance

Christmas is one occasion when a grand entrance, with music to match, is entirely appropriate. We should pull out all the stops. To this end, the procession makes far more of a dramatic impact if it suddenly appears at the main doors rather than having slunk down a side aisle, and the president and other ministers should take the trouble to make the approach by an exterior route, come rain or come shine.

'Of the Father's love begotten' takes some beating as a solemn and stately entrance hymn, or 'Once in royal David's city' if we are after something slightly more accessible. A solo voice singing the first voice of the latter is sure to tug at the heart strings, especially if the lights are dimmed and the voice sounds out in the darkness. The lights can be brought up to full as the procession enters during the second verse.

The promise of a candle-lit liturgy, though a crowd puller, is in practice of considerable nuisance value, both to the cleaning team for days afterwards and for those who may find out all too literally what it means to become a 'burning and a shining light'. A useful compromise is to save the candles for a short section of the liturgy, for example a post-communion reflection (see below). This can provide a dramatic contrast to the rest of the liturgy, while reducing the risk of the candles burning down to the cardboard holders.

Blessing of the crib

A representation of the birth scene is a traditional focus of worship for Christmastide, especially on Christmas Eve. It is customary to bless the crib, and this is best done during the procession, when the president and other ministers can pause to make a station at the crib between verses of the opening hymn. A suitable prayer of blessing is included in *Common Worship: Times and Seasons* (2006, p. 77), and, depending on local custom, holy water and incense can be used as signs of blessing and setting apart.

Greeting and hymn of praise

At the end of the opening hymn, the president greets the people, announces the theme of the day and calls upon the assembly to give thanks to God, moving straight into the hymn of praise, which can be either the *Gloria in Excelsis* or some suitable hymn such as 'Angels from the realms of glory'.

In so doing we omit the penitential rite, and this is entirely appropriate if we have kept a good Advent and have arrived, suitably prepared, for the liturgical party. The recitation of a penitential rite, either here or at a later point, would seem an unwarranted intrusion for the sake of including all the possible bits there are to include on every conceivable occasion (a frequently encountered bad habit).

Liturgy of the Word

After the Liturgy of the Word, following the homily, the short period of silence should be observed as usual, no matter how large the crowd of those to whom it will appear novel or strange. It is important for the faith community to maintain 'business as usual' in the essential elements of the liturgy, and the president can always preface the silence with an explanatory word.

Gathering at the font

After the silence, the president rises to announce the procession of the assembly to the font or baptismal pool which, after the dryness of Advent, is now once again filled to overflowing to take its place as a central focus of every liturgy until Lent. The question of the design and location of the font/baptismal pool in the planning of the whole liturgical space is treated more fully in *Re-Pitching the Tent* (Giles, 2004b). Suffice it so say here that a focus of the baptismal life around which the assembly can conveniently gather during the Sunday Liturgy (irrespective of whether or not a baptism is taking place) is a *sine qua non* of a renewed liturgical life for any community of the baptized.

In Christmastide, the penitential rite having been dispensed with, the font becomes the focus, not of penance and cleansing, but of affirming our faith. This is entirely appropriate at the liturgical place where baptism is celebrated, bearing in mind that the first versions of the Christian creed took the form of baptismal responses.

Arriving at the font, the president invites the assembly to affirm its common faith, using whatever formula the pastor thinks best, and then sprinkles the assembly with water from the font using a suitable vessel with a branch or *aspergillum,* a ceremony dating back to the ninth century. During the sprinkling, a song about the water of life is sung, or (on Christmas Eve) a carol.

Prayers of the people

The prayers of the people need to be brief and to the point on this occasion, and it is one of those (rare) times when enlisting the most creative of intercessors is not the best idea. The safest way of all is for the president, or preferably one of the other ministers of the liturgy, to offer short bidding prayers to focus the prayers of the assembly.

The sharing of the Peace

The president then introduces the Peace, using one of the excellent seasonal sentences from *Common Worship: Times and Seasons* (2006), and another minister of the liturgy invites the people to offer one another a sign of peace.

The eucharistic prayer

Even when, as on Christmas Eve, numbers are large, the assembly should nevertheless continue to be invited to surround the altar and be seen as an offering community, even if the edges become a little ragged and liturgical order unravels somewhat. The movement of the crowd to the altar table and their proximity to the centre of things is what will leave a lasting impression on participants, especially any who have not taken part in worship for some time.

The communion

The method of distributing communion may have to depend to some extent on numbers present and on what is most easily explained with least fuss. The assembly remains around the altar for communion and must also be discouraged from drifting away back to their seats once having received, and this needs to be made clear by the president before communion. The assembly should remain in place around the altar table, first because this emphasizes that the assembly is a community moving together, not a collection of individuals doing their own thing, and because, once communion is over, we have more things to do.

While the assembly is still at the altar table after communion, and while the ablutions are being carried out, hand-held candles are distributed to everyone and lit, and the lighting dimmed. The president says the post-communion prayer and then announces the procession to the crib

Visit to the crib

On the occasion of the First Mass of Christmas, the post-communion reflection, the time of quiet before we re-enter our world, should take place at the crib. The assembly follows the president and other ministers who make their way to the crib and take up positions in front of it. During the procession, an excellent hymn to sing is 'A stable lamp is lighted', the most hauntingly beautiful hymn in the Episcopal Church's *The Hymnal 1982*. At the crib, after a suitable period of silent adoration, a carol such as 'Little Jesus, sweetly sleep' or 'Away in a manger' can be sung, after which a concluding prayer, such as prayer 6 on page 95 of *Common Worship: Times and Seasons* (2006), is said by all.

Concluding rite

It is sensible to have the solemn blessings and dismissal said at the crib, where people are already gathered, and then to allow them to return to their places during the concluding hymn, while the president and ministers make their way to the main doors.

Hospitality

On such an occasion with many visitors and guests, hospitality should be offered quickly and simply as people mill around after the service. This can take place in the narthex or at the back of the worship space. A single commodity, for example spiced mulled wine in disposable tumblers, is the best way of catering for large numbers (and will be talked about for some time to come).

Christmas Morning

As discussed above, the Liturgy of Christmas Morning is essentially more theologically reflective and more focused on the Word made flesh than on the infant in the stable. The crib, having been blessed the night before, does not feature in the liturgy unless the morning service is the main event in the parish for families with young children.

The Christmas season

The length of the Christmas season is variable, and raises interesting questions. The most widespread tradition is that Christmas lasts until the feast of the Epiphany (i.e twelve days), after which we revert to Ordinary Time, the liturgical colour changing back to green.

There seems to be in some circles a growing tendency to allot a full 40 days to Christmastide, culminating in the feast of the Presentation on 2 February. As well as stretching the consumption of left-over turkey a little too far, a 40-day Christmastide, even for the most energetic party-goer, confirms the worst suspicions of the secularists who tend, in well-meaning ignorance, to commiserate with clergy on the nature of this season as 'your busiest time'.

Holy Week and Easter is of course the Church's really busy time, and by comparison Christmas is a side show. For the Church to further extend Christmastide is a risky strategy, for it suggests that Christianity stands or falls on an event for which we have no detailed historical evidence and which has for the last hundred years or so had both believer and antagonist hung up on a virgin birth and attendant wonders including genuflecting farm animals and angelic four-part choirs.

Feasts need to stand out in relief against the rest of the liturgical calendar that surrounds them. If Epiphany and the Presentation emerge from a sea of an endless Christmas they inevitably lose some of their purpose and point.

Saints in the Christmas season

It was a great privilege for Stephen, the first person to be killed for allegiance to the Jesus movement, and John, the disciple seated next to Jesus at that final meal, to be allotted the most sought-after slots in the Christian calendar immediately adjoining the Master's birthday.

Following sharply on the heels of Stephen and John come the Holy Innocents (28 December), a feast which grows ever more topical as the world dedicates ever more energy and technology in violence against the defenceless, and Thomas of Canterbury (29 December), the rightful patron saint of the Church of England once it gets its backbone reinserted. (Thomas was a magnificent king-baiter and it is small wonder that Henry VIII determined to destroy not only his shrine but his memory. Shame on the English Church for colluding with such Erastian pettiness for the last 500 years; it is high time we made restitution with a right old liturgical knees-up on 29 December.)

Sadly, however, it has turned out to be a dumb deal to be commemorated so close to the boss's birthday. As any kid can tell you whose parents got carried away in late March, it's no fun having a birthday on or around Christmas Day. Try as you might, there is no doubt that you are done out of a proper celebration in its own right. Attempting to organize on Boxing Day a really grand patronal festival in a parish dedicated to Stephen is no fun either.

Having said that, when it comes to the saints of Christmas week, all may not be lost. With the tendency for the majority of people to be off work for most of these days, a good many of whom will be looking for an excuse to slip out of the house to avoid over-exposure to visiting relatives, there is much scope for commemorating these saints in a meaningful way. These days have a special 'out of time' quality, with a sense of having stepped out for a moment from the frantic pace of the rest of the year, and this should be made the most of.

The time of day most likely to work will be late morning or midday, or perhaps, once we get to 28 or 29 December, there will be scope for something in the evening. A simple eucharist, relaxed and contemplative in style, could be followed by a short social time with refreshments, which leads, for those who wish to linger for a while, into a discussion time on the theme of the day. For Stephen this might be martyrdom, for John the contemplative dimension of the Christian life, for Holy Innocents the state of the world, and for Thomas the state of the Church.

Such occasions demand a light touch, and 'discussion group' might involve nothing more than standing around in the narthex after the eucharist, with coffee cup or sherry glass in hand, as the discussion is gently led away from how full everyone feels to matters of deeper import.

These are also good occasions to remember those for whom Christmas is a dreaded time of loneliness or isolation. This involves more than those who live alone; it is possible to be isolated in a houseful of people, especially where the spiritual dimension of life is not understood. The quiet observance of the saints of Christmas week offers many opportunities for spiritual formation for the pastor aware of the possibilities.

Christingle services

Of all writers on this subject I am the least qualified, as I have never in my life organized a Christingle service (and neither, by the way, have I ever been to Taizé). Christingle services are an amazing phenomenon. They can fill cathedrals at the drop of a hat.

Originating with the Moravian community in eighteenth-century Germany, the 'Candle Service' was a Christmas Eve service in which a lighted candle with a red ribbon was given to the children present. This evolved into the 'Christingle' (from the German 'Christ-engel': Christ-angel) which incorporated rather more ambitious symbolism perfected in England by the Children's Society who in 1968 were smart enough to make the Christingle their 'thing', and run with it.

An orange (representing the world) is the centrepiece, into which is inserted a small candle (Jesus the light of the world). A red ribbon is tied around the orange (the blood or love of Christ), and four cocktail sticks inserted in the orange with fruits or sweets on the ends (the four seasons and the fruits of the earth).

The Christingle is an interesting example of a very simple quasi-liturgical idea, albeit one demanding no little preparation, of enormous appeal to a wide audience. The visual effect of a darkened cathedral on a late Saturday afternoon in winter, lit by a thousand tiny lights lifted high by children singing a well-known carol is a spine-tingling occasion, corny though it may sound. The proof of the pudding lies in the fact that, over Christmas 2006 for example, the Children's Society raised over £1.2m from participants at these services.

This may be dismissed by some as the continuing fascination of de-Christianized Britain for folk religion, or for what we might call 'Christmas without strings' or 'Christmas lite', but the Church should capitalize on such instincts rather than simply deride them. How might we respond? How might we encounter those who come in such a way that something of the core of Christian good news is imparted, but with so light a touch that those present may realize only afterwards what has been planted in hearts and minds?

See-at-a-glance liturgy for Christmas

Chair

Entrance procession
Blessing of the crib
Greeting

Ambo

Prayer of the day
Reading from the Hebrew Scriptures
Psalm
Reading from the Christian Scriptures
Alleluia
Gospel
Procession of the Gospel Book
Homily

Silence
Song of journey

Font

Affirmation of faith
Sprinkling of the people
Prayers of the people

The Peace
Song of journey

Altar table

The eucharistic prayer
Sanctus
Lord's Prayer
Breaking of the bread
Communion
Distribution, lighting and blessing of candles

At the crib

Reflection
Post-communion prayer
Announcements
Blessing
Sending out

Music for Christmas

A typical selection of music for Christmas. See Appendix 3 for full publishing details.

Entrance song

'Once in Royal David's city'.

Psalm

Psalm 98, Gelineau, in *Lectionary Psalms*.

Alleluia

'Festival Alleluia', James Chepponis, Morning Star Publishers (sheet music).

Song of journey (to the font)

'O little town of Bethlehem' (tune: 'Forest Green'), in *The New English Hymnal* and *The Hymnal 1982*.

Sprinkling song

'Of the Father's love begotten' (tune: 'Divinum Mysterium'), in *The New English Hymnal* and *Gather*.

Song of journey (to the altar table)

'The first Noel' (tune: 'The First Nowell').

Communion

'Good Christian friends rejoice' (tune: 'In Dulce Jubilo'), in *New Hymns and Worship Songs*.
'Away in a manger', William James Kirkpatrick.

Song of journey (to the Crib)

'A stable lamp is lighted', David Hurd, in *The Hymnal 1982*.

Song at the Crib

'Silent night', Franz Xaver Grubert.

Final song

'O come, all ye faithful' (tune: Adeste fideles).

4 EPIPHANY

The Epiphany ('showing forth' or 'manifestation') of Christ is a celebration of the proclamation of the Christ to the world. This has been variously understood as (in the Church of the West) the revelation of the Christ child to the three mysterious magi/astrologers/magicians/sages from Far Eastern lands representative of the many cultures of the known world, or as (in the Church in the East) the revelation of Jesus (as a grown man) as the Christ, the Anointed of God, to the crowds seeking repentance and new life in first-century Palestine.

Historical background

The feast of the Epiphany of Christ is a case where the Church of the West took a wrong turning a very long time ago, entering a liturgical thicket from which it is now impossible to extricate itself.

The intention to draw a distinction between the recognition of the adult Jesus of Nazareth as the Christ, the Anointed One of God, and the commemoration of the (rather hazy) events surrounding his birth and infancy at Bethlehem, is common to the whole Church. Whereas in the East the showing forth was associated from the outset with the baptism of Christ, a wholly positive emphasis on the launch of Jesus' public ministry, the West preferred to lumber itself with the dubious legend (recorded only in Matthew's Gospel) of the Magi who, following a star, made their way to Bethlehem to pay their respects to a Christ Child of indeterminate age, and managed to get rather a lot of children killed while they were at it.

Characteristics

The themes of Epiphany – light, recognition, showing forth, anointing, and commissioning for public ministry – are wholly positive, accessible and well suited to liturgical creativity.

The baptism of an adult catechumen

Coming as it does between Advent and Lent, the period associated with Epiphany majors on light rather than darkness, affirmation rather than penance, and the shadow of the cross has not yet fallen across the picture.

Pastorally and strategically, Epiphany is a highly appropriate time for commissioning new ministries and for inaugurating new initiatives in social action and mission.

Even if one concentrates merely on the less demanding and more folksy emphasis of the Magi story, Epiphany offers something of a respite from the grim foreboding of all that must inevitably follow.

Cultural context

The end result of associating the Epiphany with the coming of the Magi is of course that Epiphany (in the West) gets intertwined with Christmas. 'The first noel' is the most obvious example of an Epiphany carol hijacked for Christ's birthday celebrations, and the purist who attempts to avoid Christmas cards adorned with three gurus on a camel pointing to a star embraces a lost cause.

Moreover, the Baptism of Christ is reduced to a single Sunday instead of informing a whole season, and Epiphanytide is simply a season of nibbling on liturgical leftovers.

In fact the concept of an Epiphanytide season is itself a dubious notion, but has grown like Topsy with the passing of the years. It now calls forth in both Roman and Anglican communions bouts of liturgical schizophrenia. Epiphany originally had no octave or season attached to it, and the Sundays that followed it were an odd collection of bits and pieces filling in the gap until Lent. This included a number of Sundays after Epiphany, varying in number depending on when Easter was due to fall, and the three Sundays before Lent bearing until 1969 (in Rome) and 1980 (in the Church of England) the wonderfully quaint names of Septuagesima, Sexagesima, and Quinquagesima, referring approximately to the number of days before Easter.

These Sundays between Epiphany and Lent have in both communions always been ordinary green Sundays, and with the liturgical reforms arising out of Vatican II Rome regularized their ordinariness by calling them 'Sundays in Ordinary Time'. At the same time, the figures of the Magi are often found remaining in place until the feast of the Presentation of Christ on 2 February, and there is an increasing tendency to prolong the festal garb of Christmas/Epiphany until that feast.

In the Church of England however, as in the Episcopal Church of the USA, 'Epiphanytide' is more and more spoken of as a season, and *Common Worship: Times and Seasons* (2006) speaks of the period up to the Presentation as this 'season of joyful celebration' and 'festal cycle' (p. 120). This despite the fact that the Sundays are numbered *after* Epiphany and not *of* it, and remain green, except of course for the first after Epiphany which is always now a white Sunday for the Baptism of Christ.

The choice of gospel readings for these Sundays reveals something of the dilemma, the Revised Common Lectionary, especially Year C, continuing the Epiphany theme with incidents developing the motif of manifestation such as the wedding at Cana and Jesus' declaration of intent at the synagogue at Nazareth.

The Church of the West is therefore not only liable to get liturgically confused in this season, but is also greatly impoverished theologically, continuing to base our understanding of Christ's showing forth to the nations in terms of sensational events surrounding his birth and infancy, rather than on his anointing by the Spirit of God and his subsequent public ministry. Perhaps many of the christological controversies of later centuries started here, at this early fork in the liturgical road.

Be that as it may, and until the great schism of 1054 CE is healed, we must make do with what we have. We can do so by approaching the celebration of Christ's showing forth as a mystery in two parts: first on 6 January the Coming of the Magi, and then on the Sunday following the Coming of the Spirit on Christ in Baptism.

The Coming of the Magi should always be celebrated on the day, not the nearest Sunday. This ensures that the Baptism of Christ (that is, Epiphany as understood in the Church of the East) is given precedence in the Sunday experience of the regular church member. We can do our best with the Coming of the Magi on 6 January, majoring on the symbolic significance of this persevering band of seers and sages from exotic eastern lands, and their ethnic diversity (the author of Matthew could never have guessed how useful *that* would be). It is a good festival for involving children, and for this reason also, a weekday celebration of this feast, with opportunities for working with local schools, is to be preferred.

Bearing in mind that the Holy Family, if they hung around Bethlehem at all, no doubt in time graduated from the stable to some temporary accommodation, why not construct a different symbolic home for the young child Jesus as distinct from the stable where the shepherds came to adore the infant? This could be located in a different part of the worship space. This makes the point visually that we are here dealing with an event quite separate from Christmas, with a quite separate theological meaning.

The Coming of the Spirit on Christ in Baptism, celebrated on the Sunday following, gives us a far more wholesome and constructive emphasis for the showing forth of Christ, with a far more solid scriptural and theological foundation. This day is really pure joy for the homilist intent on building up in the Body of Christ a sense of God's special purpose and sending forth. The Church serves it up on a plate for us to take and delight in.

The length of 'Epiphanytide', as it is now often called, presents something of a problem. It is a green season, and for crib figures or festal decorations of any kind to remain in place throughout the many weeks following the feast is plainly inappropriate. There is a case for continuing some special decorations until the feast of the Presentation of Christ on 2 February, but not much of a case. The more we come to emphasize the Eastern Church's understanding of Epiphany as anointing, baptism and sending forth, the more we shall want to move on beyond the fabulous stories surrounding Christ's infancy, and engage with the public ministry of Jesus of Nazareth. In this way we too may learn how to take up our cross and follow him. Liturgically, we shall be itching to move from white to green, and to get on with things.

The very last Sunday in Epiphanytide, or the last before Lent, poses a problem of a different kind, arising from the readings set in the Revised Common Lectionary. These focus on the theme of transfiguration, with the appointed Gospel describing the transfiguration of Jesus on the mountain. This makes excellent sense in its liturgical context, reminding us, just before Lent begins, of the true identity of he who is about to set his face towards Jerusalem.

Human nature being what it is, however, we find those responsible for leading worship all too often referring to this Sunday as 'Transfiguration Sunday' when it is nothing of the sort. Some even go so far as to don white vestments (allowed for as an alternative in the Episcopal Church, believe it or not) and treat it as a feast day, when all the time it is a dear old ordinary green Sunday. The feast of the Transfiguration is of course 6 August, and just because a large proportion of the faithful will be down at the beach in August is no excuse for vandalizing the Church's Year with a pseudo-feast in the middle of February.

Choreography

Setting

For the feast itself on 6 January, it is customary for figures of the Magi to be placed in the liturgical space as reminders of the Matthean story of their journey to adore the Christ Child. Tradition has it that this event took place some while after the birth, and an effort should be made to distinguish symbolically the place of adoration from that of the shepherds at the birth of Jesus. This gives the feast at least some semblance of a distinct character and purpose of its own.

Figures of the Magi, perhaps even made by members of the faith community in a workshop project, can be carried in procession, placed in the holy house, and blessed.

Orientation

Epiphany provides a good opportunity for a seating plan that looks outwards rather than inwards, and which both embraces the newcomer and causes the regular member to look beyond the familiar and the immediate towards the horizons of God's domain. In such ways is the proclamation of Christ to the world modelled by the way we assemble for worship.

One configuration which has an Epiphany ring about it is that of the parish of St Gregory of Nyssa, San Francisco, which in many ways reverses the normal routine. Traditionally one enters a liturgical space through the 'soft' zone of the word, moving gradually to the 'sacred' zone of the altar table, a progression which speaks of levels of participation for those ritually initiated.

At St Gregory's, this pattern is put back to front, so that the altar table is encountered in the large gathering space immediately adjoining the main doors, with the place of the word beyond it, further into the heart of the building complex. This arrangement achieves two significant adjustments to our customary thinking.

Epiphany: layout of liturgical space

First, the newcomer is on arrival brought face to face with a table laid for a meal, rather than an altar in a distant sanctuary. In this way a symbol of open hospitality replaces one of a ritualized mystique.

Second, the whole assembly is, at the conclusion of the liturgy, as it were propelled directly from the eucharistic table into the surrounding streets. It is a eucharistic rite in which the dismissal is a genuine commissioning to social action and compassionate involvement. The coffee hour that inevitably, and quite rightly, intervenes between dismissal and hitting the streets, is in itself harnessed to the liturgy's didactic purpose, the coffee urn being placed, immediately after the dismissal, on the same table where the sacred elements have just been taken, blessed, broken and shared. In this way we are reminded that the line between sacred and regular food is a hazy and indistinct one; both are part of God's abundant providence.

Although few of us are in the position of building a new liturgical space around our theology, as was the case at St Gregory's, nevertheless we may have spaces flexible enough to allow some experimentation along these lines. Simply reversing the normal positions of altar table and ambo will in itself provide sufficient 'shock therapy' to jolt us out of the predictable into a renewed sense of journey into the unknown.

Liturgical furniture

At Epiphany it is the font that takes pride of place, the focus of the assembly's attention as we identify ourselves with ritual cleansing and anointing by the Spirit.

If the font in our liturgical space is not up to the job, or badly sited, every effort should be made to make special arrangements for the Baptism of Christ and the Sundays after Epiphany that follow. If the existing font can be made to work but is badly sited, it should be relocated to a place where it achieves liturgical prominence. Where this is not possible, space should be cleared around it so that the assembly can make it a 'station' in the procession of the liturgical action.

If neither options are available, or even if they are, the existing font should be temporarily decommissioned, and a large temporary font, or better still a pool, constructed in a place which leaves no room for doubt as to what is central in our thinking in this season. A children's paddling pool, suitably camouflaged with large stones, would even do the job.

Eucharistic liturgy

Entrance

In recognition of the joyous significance of the revelation of Jesus as God's Anointed, now presented to the world, the note struck at the beginning of the liturgy in Epiphanytide should be triumphal and celebratory.

Unlike Ordinary Time, the liturgical ministers will enter in procession, to the accompaniment of a suitably strong and joyful hymn or song. After the greeting, the president outlines the theme of the day and introduces the song of praise, which might be the *Gloria* or contemporary equivalent.

After the Liturgy of the Word, and a time of silence, the assembly moves in joyful procession to the font, there to affirm their faith in the One who was baptized and sent forth, as are they.

Gathering at the font

In no liturgical season is the gathering at the font of more symbolic significance (apart from at the Easter Vigil itself) than during these Sundays after Epiphany. On the first Sunday after the feast itself we celebrate the Baptism of Christ and rejoice in the fact that we too have been brought to the waters of repentance and renewal.

Christ is a teacher and master who leads by example, and we take delight in being associated so closely and precisely with him in this little death that leads to life. We learn that, in Christ, we too become God's beloved ones, with whom God is well pleased.

In the Sundays that follow, we are shown the direct connection between the font and the market place; between Jesus' commissioning as God's Anointed One and his immersion in public ministry. In the Gospel accounts that the liturgy presents to us in these weeks, we are brought face to face with the confrontation inherent in the release of God's gracious power among humankind, and the upheaval that must inevitably follow. If we have ears to hear and eyes to see, we are in these weeks trained in costly discipleship.

It is no bad thing to ring the changes between seasons when it comes to the penitential rite. If so, the positive emphasis of Epiphany as proclamation might cause us to omit the penitential rite during the Sundays of Epiphany, bearing in mind that Lent will soon give us more than enough penance. That being the case, we gather at the font at this different point in the liturgy and with a different purpose.

As we gather around the waters of baptism, recalling our own baptismal vows, we make an affirmation of faith, and rededicate ourselves in ministry and service.

A form of affirmation based on the baptismal formula is particularly appropriate, an example of which might be:

Do you believe and trust in God the creator, source of all being and life, the one for whom we exist?
We believe and trust in God.
Do you believe and trust in God the liberator, who shared our human existence, and showed us how to live, and die?
We believe and trust in God.
Do you believe and trust in God the sustainer, who gives life to the people of God, and makes Christ known to the world?
We believe and trust in God.
This is the faith of the Church.
This is our faith. We believe in one God, creator, liberator and sustainer.

Following the affirmation of faith, the president sprinkles the assembly with baptismal water, using a branch and a suitable container of water scooped from the font. By way of introduction, the president recalls the assembly to its baptismal covenant which is symbolically renewed in this liturgical action.

The sprinkling should be accompanied by one of the many songs on the theme of water, available from several sources. Paul Inwood's 'Waters of new birth', or Marty Haughen's 'Springs of water', or Robert Buckley Farlee's 'O Blessed Spring'.[1] The president should take care to note the length of the piece and to pace the sprinkling accordingly. All too often the president gallops around the assembly at a furious pace, only to have to wait out in fidgety inactivity the remaining verses of the song.

At the completion of the sprinkling, the prayers of the people follow, and these should be led from the font also, in the midst of the assembly encircling the baptismal pool.

The sharing of the Peace which follows the prayers of the people is also announced at the font, for the waters of baptism make a most fitting point of origin from which to set out to make reconciliation. Like the fountain in the town square, the font is the place of meeting, encounter and starting again.

Procession to the altar table

The assembly, having shared the Peace, moves forward as a body to stand around the altar table.

The eucharistic prayer

The assembly encircles the altar table, with the president standing at the head of the table, but nevertheless as part of the circle, not out of it or over and above it.

Dismissal

Epiphany is a season when we might want to think of ways of making explicit the connection between our sending forth from the liturgy and our engagement with the world. This is one reason why the altar table might be placed for this season near the exit rather than furthest away from it, facilitating a symbolic movement direct from the liturgy into the world around us.

In real life we know full well that this means in most cases a movement direct from dismissal not to the street but to coffee hour, but as we have seen with the example of St Gregory's, San Francisco (p. 61 above), even the arrangements for coffee hour can be brought into the overall theological framework of a well thought out liturgy. Everything we do as the assembly of God's people, from the moment we enter the building to the moment we leave, is part of our formation as the Body of Christ, a formation in which the old distinctions between 'sacred' and 'secular' no longer pertain.

Feast of the Presentation

Character

During the dark, damp days of early February, the feast of the Presentation of Christ in the Temple, traditionally called Candlemas, is sent as blessed relief from gloom. It is an innocent little festival, mercifully free from ponderous theological overtones, marking the Holy Family's conformity to Jewish practice regarding a firstborn son; the equivalent of a christening party today.

For a feast celebrating a small ritual incident, the Presentation is extremely rich in sacred textual material, all of it from St Luke's Gospel (2.22–39), covering not only the bringing of the child to Jerusalem with the offering proscribed by the Mosaic Law, but also two significant encounters: first with the holy man Simeon who took the child in his arms, blessed him, and exclaimed the song of praise that bears his name, and with the prophet Anna, who also praised God for him.

Historical background

This feast has come a long way in a short time. In the *Book of Common Prayer* (1662) the feast's primary name is the Purification of the Blessed Virgin Mary, with the Presentation of Christ as the alternative in smaller print. This emphasis on purification can be traced back to the Hebraic view (Leviticus 12) that childbirth rendered the mother unclean, as did the menstrual cycle, a concept still lurking in the rites of the first English Prayer Books, despite more positive language and a new title, 'The Thanksgiving of Women after Child-Birth commonly called the Churching of Women'.

This emphasis on purification was, however, a hang-up of the Western Church. In contrast, healthier attitudes prevailed in the Church of the East, where the feast first became widespread in the sixth century after being promoted by the Emperor Justinian; it had the charming name of 'The Meeting' (that is, between Christ and Simeon). This was not just a meeting between generations, but between worlds – of the old dispensation and the new.

It was during this meeting that Simeon, with the child in his arms, let rip with his song 'Master, now you are dismissing your servant in peace', known traditionally as the Nunc Dimittis from the first two words of the opening line in Latin. The song's acclamation of the child Jesus as 'a light for revelation to the Gentiles' gave rise to the blessing and distribution of candles on this day, hence 'Candlemas'.

Cultural context

It is astonishing today to consider that as late as the 1950s in industrial parishes of our major cities the service for the Churching of Women was still advertised in the parish magazine, many women who had given birth remaining anxious about being seen in public until they had gone to be 'churched'.

More wholesome attitudes found their place in the church calendar in the wake of Vatican II, both Rome and Canterbury dropping all mention of purification in the reformed liturgical texts that followed. This move away from uncleanness of childbirth also involved shifting the spotlight, quite properly, from Mary to Christ. It is now regarded as a feast of the Lord, rather than of the Lord's mother.

This swing back to the centrality of Jesus in this celebration is a return to the primitive emphasis after many centuries during which devotion to Mary took us to some extent off track (to perpetuate the negative emphasis on childbirth as essentially unclean was considered a price worth paying).

Choreography

The feast of the Presentation deserves better treatment than it usually receives. When it falls on a weekday it is often celebrated at whatever time there might be a regular eucharist that day, instead of after dark when the candles can come into their own. It warrants more of an effort on our part, as it is a feast which is both tactile and full of meaning at many levels.

The assembly should gather, not in the liturgical space, but in another building or room nearby. After lighting the candles, the presider gives a short homily explaining the significance of this day, and blesses the candles. The assembly then moves in procession to the main liturgical space, singing the Song of Simeon. There are many fine contemporary versions of this, for example Christopher Walker's 'Nunc Dimittis'.

In the Liturgy of the Word, ways should be explored of drawing out the theme of 'meeting', between young and old, the ancient order and the new. The appealing characters of Simeon and Anna are a gift for any dramatist ready to draw from the Lucan account its potential for theatre. Luke's account of how Simeon, 'guided by the Holy Spirit, came into the temple', and Anna, lurking in the shadows, who 'at that moment' appeared out of nowhere, are stage directions in themselves.

See-at-a-glance liturgy of Epiphanytide

Chair

Entrance – processional hymn
Greeting
Song of praise

Ambo

Prayer of the day
Reading form the Hebrew Scriptures
Psalm
Reading from the Christian Scriptures
Alleluia
Gospel
Procession of Gospel Book
Homily

Silence

Song of journey

Font

Affirmation of faith
Sprinkling
Prayers of the people

The Peace
Song of journey

Altar table

Song of offering
The eucharistic prayer
Sanctus
Lord's Prayer
Fraction
Communion
Invitation to reflection

Ambo

Silence

Song of reflection
Post-communion prayer
Announcements
Sending out

Music for Epiphanytide

See Appendix 3 for full publishing details.

Song of praise

'O splendour of God's glory bright' (tune: 'Splendor paternae gloriae'), plainsong, in *The Hymnal 1982*.

Psalm

'Happy are they' (Psalm 119), Peter Hallock, *The Ionian Psalter*.

Alleluia

'Festival Alleluia', James Chepponis, OCP Publications (sheet music).

Song of journey (to the font)

'We shall draw water joyfully', Paul Inwood, in *The Complete Celebration Hymnal* and *Journeysongs*.

Sprinkling song

'God our fountain of salvation', Christopher Walker, in *Journeysongs*.

Song of journey (to the altar table)

'From the East and West, from the North and South', The Collegeville Composers Group, in *Psallite: Sacred Song for Liturgy and Life*.

Communion

'One bread, one body', John Foley, in *Celebration Hymnal for Everyone* and *Gather*.
'You satisfy the hungry heart', Tobert E. Kreutz, in *Breaking Bread Hymnal* and *Gather*.

Song of reflection

'God beyond all names', Bernadette Farrell, in *Breaking Bread Hymnal* and *Celebration Hymnal for Everyone*.
'The love of God comes close', John Bell, Wild Goose Publications (sheet music).

Final song

'The people that in darkness sat', Perry Dundee, *Hymns Ancient and Modern Revised*.

Notes

1 Paul Inwood, 'Waters of new life' in *Ritual Moments: Music for Sacraments, RCIA and Other Occasions* (Chicago IL: GIA Publications, 2005). Marty Haugan, 'Springs of water', from his Mass setting *Beneath the Tree of Life* (Chicago IL: GIA Publications, 2000). Robert Buckley Farlee, 'O Blessed Spring', in *Wonder, Love and Praise* (New York: Church Publishing Inc., 1997).

5 LENT

Lent is the 40-day penitential period leading up to Easter during which the Christian Church prepares itself anew to walk with Jesus of Nazareth through his betrayal, execution and resurrection. Lent is a period of testing and trial, lasting a symbolic forty days, between his baptism and the launch of his public ministry.

Historical background

Interestingly, Lent may well have been attached originally to Epiphany and the Baptism of Jesus, which would have enjoyed complete scriptural warranty in that the temptations in the wilderness followed immediately his anointing by the Spirit in baptism: 'The Spirit immediately drove him out into the wilderness. And he was in the wilderness forty days, tempted by Satan' (Mark 1.12–13).

Like a shifting continent, however, Lent somehow became disconnected from Epiphany and drifted across the liturgical ocean to become firmly affixed to Easter. This was probably a quite inevitable development, as human nature abhors, as well as a vacuum, the thought of hardship without a *terminus ad quem*. If we are going to beat ourselves up, we will need to see some light at the end of the tunnel; a pint at the pub at the end of the all-day hike. Lent therefore demands its Easter, and the drama and pathos of Holy Week, leading into the joyous climax of Easter Day, provides a glorious culmination to the dogged penitential journey that would be the envy of Hollywood.

Coupling Lent to Easter also gave the Church the opportunity to extend the fast into a 40-day period by which the individual penitent could identify his/her struggle to remain constantly alert to God with that of Jesus himself in his 40-day sojourn in the desert.

The coupling of Lent to Easter provided a ready-made and clearly defined preparation time for those to be admitted or readmitted to the Church at the Easter ceremonies of Christian initiation. This involved both new catechumens and those who had been excluded from the Church's life and worship by reason of grievous sin. This accounts for the emphasis on self-examination, fasting, penitence and spiritual discipline which have traditionally been associated with this season.

A natural further development was the involvement of the whole Christian community in this process of prayerful and disciplined preparation, by way of solidarity with those to go through the rites of initiation, in what has become a kind of annual 'refresher course' for all Christians. Significantly, this period of training and preparation is now the common property of every Christian tradition, whether liturgical or not.

Characteristics

Lent begins on Ash Wednesday, six and a half weeks before Easter Day, though this was not always the case. Until the seventh century, Lent began on Quadragesima Sunday (what we now call Lent 1), and this remains the case in the Ambrosian Rite enshrining the ancient customs of the church in Milan. The adding of the four extra days was a clever bit of liturgical skullduggery; a change which, though appearing to prolong the fast, in fact lessened its demands by creating space for days off. The change to Ash Wednesday gave us a Lenten fast precisely 40 days long provided you excluded the Sundays (just in case anyone tended to take this whole fasting thing too seriously).

Over time, the Church's rules governing the observance of Lent have inevitably softened. In the early centuries the observance was strict – one meal a day, taken toward evening – and was embraced by all the devout. As time passed, however, the hour of the day when food could be taken each day was pushed earlier and earlier, and the number of fasting days within Lent steadily reduced. By the time of Vatican II, the Lenten fast was in effect reduced to just the first day of Lent and Good Friday.

Lent is the primary penitential season of the Church's Year. It is made of sterner stuff than Advent, and provides us with a season when it is generally understood that we get down to some serious business. The origin of Lent lies in the countdown training period for baptismal candidates at Easter, but was gradually widened into a period of spiritual limbering up for all. Lent meets the human need to balance self-indulgence with an occasional burst of restraint, and builds on the Christian's desire (albeit only in manageable chunks) to enter into the wilderness experience of Jesus.

Cultural context

Among the seasons of the Church's Year, Lent is ironically the one most widely recognized, if not understood, by the person in the street. 'Though I have drifted a long way from the fervent attachment that bound me to the C of E throughout my childhood,' wrote *The Times* columnist Jane Shilling, 'the old thread still twitches a bit, especially during the church year's two great periods of self-examination and repentance, Lent and Advent' (26 January 2007). No matter how residual Christianity becomes in Western society, everyone knows that in Lent one gives up things and generally tries to avoid excess, even if the reason for such attempts at self-discipline have long been forgotten.

There is general acceptance that during Lent things will change. The worship space will look different, parts of the liturgy will be omitted, and the whole ethos will be one of restraint and minimalism.

There are no flowers in the liturgical space, and musical excess is reined in. In addition, Lent covers a multitude of sins in that it provides a very useful excuse for harassed clergy to say 'no' to all kinds of things, from weddings to raffles.

Lent, above all other seasons, is a time when the Church's liturgy and personal devotions and self-disciplines go hand in hand. There is widespread acceptance, both inside and outside the Church, of the notion of keeping oneself in check for the period of Lent as a means of developing self-control, albeit disguised as merely a desire to lose weight or preserve one's teeth.

In the contemporary post-Christian culture we inhabit, when it is difficult enough for people to assemble for worship on a Sunday let alone on a weekday evening, it is perhaps surprising that the Church has clung to the custom of beginning Lent on a Wednesday. Given the trend in some quarters towards moving certain feasts to the nearest Sunday, we may well have imagined that the launch of Lent would have gone the same way.

Ash Wednesday, along with Good Friday, is prescribed in the American *Book of Common Prayer* (1979) as a major fast day, and in *Common Worship* (2000) is named a principal holy day. In the Roman Church Ash Wednesday and Good Friday are the only two universally prescribed fast days which survive.

Although it is usually still possible, given our inbuilt sense of Augustinian unworthiness, to raise a fair crowd for this annual launch of the penitential open season, and for the series of devotional or formational extras which usually follow, getting down to the nitty-gritty is a different matter.

If we approach Ash Wednesday correctly, that is, already stripped down and ready to dive in, then there will be a certain exhilaration in this new beginning with God, planting our feet in the footprints of Christ across the trackless desert. This is the spirit we need to encourage in the proper observance of this holy fast, and to achieve this we are given in Christian tradition the previous day, set aside for the act of getting ready. Sadly we seem to miss the point here.

Say 'Shrove Tuesday' to the average church member today, and the image that springs to mind will inevitably be a pancake supper in the parish hall, or (for those perhaps with greater social pretensions) a Mardi Gras extravaganza of some kind. As we all know, however, the origin of the name of Shrove Tuesday lies in the 'shriving' of Christians on that day, that is, their making confession and receiving absolution. The pancake race down the High Street of Olney, Buckinghamshire, was an ingenious detour to avoid the road mapped out for us by our spiritual forebears, and we should be aware of the time and sense of purpose lost in making that evasive tactic.

It is a great pity that the old squabbles of the Reformation period should cause anyone to shrink from the sacrament of reconciliation properly understood and practised, as in the Anglican tradition, as an open conversation with God with a priest alongside (not through a grille) as confidant, adviser and messenger of God's reassurance.

It is a consistent feature of the history of ritual practices that sooner or later the tail wags the dog. The day that included the preparations for a significant period of fasting and prayer now acquires greater significance than that for which it paves the way. Mardi Gras ('Fat Tuesday') in the popular mind spells partying while the going is good, making whoopee before it is too late.

The exact reason why time is allegedly running out is now for many people lost in the mists of residual folk religion. Attendance at the pancake supper may well exceed that at the Ash Wednesday services without which the previous partying has no purpose or meaning. It is Halloween and All Saints' Day all over again.

Choreography

Setting

Lent is pre-eminently the time when we should contrive to find ways of making a dramatic impact in the arrangement of our liturgical space so as to delineate this season as a very distinct period in our journey through the Church's Year. The details don't matter so much as the need to be dramatically different. No one should be left in any doubt that we have entered another, quite different, stage of the journey.

Lent: the cross is central in the liturgical space

It will be helpful if the setting of worship can be radically altered to announce the season. How exactly an impact is made will depend on the architectural character of the space and the scope it offers to ring the changes. Sometimes the building's interior fittings will give us a flying start. As a student in Newcastle I sometimes worshipped at St Gabriel's, Heaton, where the arrival of Lent was trumpeted in dramatic fashion by the closing of the doors of the huge triptych which dominated the east end of the space. The gilded figures of Christ, his apostles and saints, were suddenly gone from view, replaced by a plain façade of dull red, inscribed with the signs of the passion. Lent had arrived and everyone noticed.

We are not often, however, given such a helping hand, and must struggle to make our own liturgical waves. Visual change can be brought about by textile hangings, art work, or banners, but care should be taken to clearly establish with all concerned that such insertions into the liturgical space are purely temporary. The use of art is particularly effective in establishing the liturgical character of a season, and is a means whereby artists in the local community can be nurtured. Provided that care is taken in selecting the art, and in agreeing beforehand terms and conditions, including insurance cover, this should be a positive experience for both artist and assembly. An example of art work helping to change the liturgical mood of a large liturgical space was the display of Gerard di Falco's *Christ crucified and the solar eclipse* above the presbyterium of Philadelphia Cathedral during Lent 2007, replaced by his resurrection triptych in Eastertide.

As far as seating plans go, the particular configuration developed for Lent hardly matters; the exact shape is secondary to the need to make a difference. This can be achieved by, for example, creating a circular seating plan around the focus of the altar table placed centrally, with the ambo off to one side, balanced by the chair placed on the opposite side of the circle.

Lent: the eucharistic assembly gathered around the table

During Lent (as in Advent) the font should be drained as a sign of the wilderness experience sharpening our thirst for God. A sign should be positioned near the font to explain this and draw out the meaning of this intentional liturgical deprivation. This might read:

LENT
The season of Lent,
recalls the forty days spent by Jesus in the desert, fasting and praying.
For us too it is a time of preparation, prayer and fasting:
a wilderness time.
For this reason the font is
drained during Lent,
as a sign of
our thirsting and our emptiness.

'Blessed are those who hunger and thirst for righteousness,
for they will be filled' (Matthew 5.6).

As noted in Advent, the habit of draping swatches of material, in the liturgical colour, over and around the empty font can appear unnecessarily fussy and is best avoided.

The circular plan and the temporary removal of the font from liturgical consideration make for a more static liturgy, which in many ways may seem strange in Lent, a time which we often think of as a journey. In another sense, however, Lent can be seen as a pause in the journey when we can take stock and assess how we are doing, a temporary resting place at which the travellers gather their wagons into a circle and hunker down around the campfire.

The circular configuration is helpful in expressing this approach to Lent. Movement can be incorporated by inviting the assembly, in the period of silence after the communion, to disperse freely throughout the liturgical space for a time of individual reflection. This period of reflection may include a short meditation, or some music, or the silence may be allowed to speak for itself.

Liturgical colour

As far as the liturgical colour for Lent goes, purple immediately springs to mind, as decreed by the Western Church, and by my first vicar provided it was red purple and never 'Cadbury's Milk Tray' (although, tell it not in Gath, rumours are rife of the return of the latter).

Nothing, however, can compare with the restrained dignity of Lenten array (or sackcloth), the alternative preferred in the ancient Sarum use of pre-Reformation England. It is never a bad thing for Anglicans to recall our life before the Tudors, and thereby make a distinct and unique contribution to the liturgical life of the worldwide Church.

Altars decked in bleached Lenten array, sometimes decorated with the symbols of the passion in black and red, can be simply beautiful, as well as bearing a direct, clear and easily understood message for the assembly about Lent as a time for 'sackcloth and ashes'.

Liturgical restraint

Lent is a time in general for restraint in all quarters: subdued music, the omission of the Gloria and of Alleluia, the absence of flowers. The purists would have us forego the organ altogether, although that is taking things a bit far, especially if it would mean doing without the Kyrie of the *Missa de Angelis*, for example, the high melancholy content of which makes it highly suitable for Lent, although so exquisite as to be positively sinful. Ways should be found, however, of marking musically the transition into the Lenten season, perhaps by a reduced music list, the omission of an organ voluntary at the end, and a more limited palette of musical colours.

Music

As always, care should be taken to choose music that matches the mood of the season. For an entrance procession, it is often assumed that the Litany contained in our various books of common prayer will be most suitable, but by far the best for this purpose is the Lent Prose (*Attende Domine*), the ancient hymn of the Church in Lenten mode, dating from the sixth century. A contemporary translation can be found in *Celebration Hymnal for Everyone* (see Appendix 3 for details).

As already mentioned, the Kyrie from the *Missa de Angelis* fits the mood of Lent exactly, and can be made the striking centrepiece of the penitential rite if prefaced by suitable petitions and responses followed by a time of silence. The Kyries then follow (sung by all), after which the general absolution is pronounced. In this way, we ensure that the Kyries are an expression of our sorrowful penitence, not merely a performance of beautiful music; they are made to work for their living.

In Lent we are denied the usual array of gospel Alleluias with which to acclaim the words of Christ, and we must dig around for less celebratory alternatives. One such is Bernadette Farrell's 'Praise to you, O Christ our Saviour, word of the Father, calling us to life', which has fine words and a strong upbeat rhythm.

In this season also we may wish to simplify our musical fare by using seasonal songs or chants which we can repeat every Sunday. A good example of such material is Margaret Rizza's 'Silent, surrendered', a hauntingly beautiful hymn of merely six lines easily learned in four parts by any assembly. This is another possibility as a gospel acclamation, or it could be used as we prepare the table, or at communion.

At the end of the liturgy, there should be no final hymn or organ music to play us out. The liturgical ministers should leave in silence, the assembly remaining standing. Afterwards the assembly should be seated for a few moments, keeping the silence, and savouring the difference of this season of reflection from all other times in the Church's Year. In these little ways do we remember the difference and recall ourselves to our serious intent of closer conformity to Christ.

Ash Wednesday Liturgy

Ashing

Hidden away at the beginning of Lent is one of those little jokes which Our Lord just occasionally plays on the Church, as he pops out of the pages of the Gospel to disturb our cosy little arrangements. The Gospel passage from Matthew appointed for Ash Wednesday could not be more specific in laying before us the dominical insistence on inner authenticity not outward show. In particular the eucharistic assembly is reminded that 'whenever you fast, do not look dismal, like the hypocrites, for they disfigure their faces so as to show others they are fasting' (Matthew 6.16).

How utterly fascinating it is therefore to behold the ways in which the Church, like some recalcitrant teenager, sets out to do the exact opposite. From the earliest centuries Ash Wednesday was the day penitents were ceremoniously admitted to begin their penance. Originally restricted to 'celebrity sinners' doing public penance, from the tenth century onwards, when that custom fell into disuse, it came to involve whole congregations. Such public penance was symbolized by the imposition of ashes upon the forehead, a symbol arising from the 'sackcloth and ashes' inseparable from penitence throughout the Hebrew Scriptures.

This rite of the imposition of ashes is still prescribed in the Liturgy of Ash Wednesday in the Roman rite, and for Anglicans the use of ashes on this day continues to be a badge of honour for all who value their Catholic heritage.

So here we find ourselves on this day, ritually expressing our penitence and sorrow to God in the name of Christ who expressly forbad such outward displays of piety. It may always give us a thrill to see people on the streets on Ash Wednesday bearing the marks of their attendance at the liturgy of the day (especially prevalent in American society) and to feel solidarity with a great army of fellow believers, but it remains indefensible for any thinking Christian. It inevitably gives rise, sooner or later, to some challenging questions to presiding clergy at the church door.

So what can be done? How can we remain faithful to the teaching of Christ and to the cherished customs of our faith tradition at the same time? One possibility is to bless and administer ashes in the usual way after the homily, but then to invite, at the sharing of the Peace, all those who received ashes to wipe them from the forehead of their neighbour as a sign of forgiveness and reconciliation. In this way we can have the best of both worlds, keeping both our scriptural and liturgical integrity intact, while at the same time entering into a tactile recognition of one's interrelatedness in the Body of Christ, rather than grovelling in the private mud of individual unworthiness.

The blessing and imposition of ashes is now for Anglicans a far less clandestine affair tinged with naughtiness. Liturgical disloyalty is no longer required. As well as the form of blessing provided in the Roman Missal, both *Common Worship: Times and Seasons* and the *Book of Occasional Services* of the Episcopal Church provide excellent liturgical material with which to bring this ceremony out into the open.

Customarily, the ashes make most sense if made from the palm crosses from the previous year brought to the church and burned, although the pressures of parish life all too often mean that we remember to announce this just as people have gone home on the last Sunday before Lent begins.

Fasting

Over and above the ritual observance of Ash Wednesday in the ceremony of ashing, the real significance of the day lies in its being one of the two main fast days (together with Good Friday) of the Church's Year. Fasting is a time-hallowed means, in almost all faith traditions, of sharpening spiritual awareness by reining in bodily appetites. Fasting was part and parcel of Jewish religious observance, and the Christian Scriptures attest to its prevalence among the disciples of John the Baptizer. More importantly, fasting is commended by Jesus himself, both by example (his fast in the desert following his baptism) and in teaching (Mark 2.20).

Paul likened the spiritual life to the athlete's training programme by which he/she develops a body which is a lean and mean machine to succeed at overcoming the challenges ahead: 'So I do not run aimlessly, nor do I box as though beating the air; but I punish my body and enslave it, so that after proclaiming to others I myself should not be disqualified' (1 Corinthians 9.26–27). Despite the current popularity of the gym, such talk does not sit well with today's emphasis on personal fulfilment, and gives rise to fears of suppressing or sublimating natural desires.

The current climate of giving free rein to our personal needs is, however, exactly why fasting assumes a greater significance in our own generation than ever before, and why we should strive to make sense of it in our Ash Wednesday patterns of observance. We should seek ways of encouraging the practice of abstaining from solid food during the day (which won't kill any of us) by making a communal event out of the breaking of the fast.

For example, a Liturgy of Ash Wednesday celebrated in the early evening could be followed by a bread and soup meal perhaps leading into the launch of a Lent course of instruction. In this way the taking of food together on this night unites the faithful in a welcome respite after a tough opening section of the journey, and in a growing sense of adventure as Lent begins. In a strange kind of way, it starts (dare we say?) to be fun.

Devotional rites – stations of the cross

The stations of the cross is a devotional exercise in which the participant is enabled spiritually to follow in the footsteps of Christ on the path from his arrest to his death and burial.

The devotion originated in Jerusalem, where pilgrims were able literally to follow the route taken by our Lord. Although dating from earliest times, it did not become widespread across the Church until the fourteenth century when the Franciscans were given custody of the holy places, and set to with a will to internationalize this local custom.

Considering the universality of stations these days, worshippers have shown remarkably little creativity in bringing this devotional exercise to life. Although traditionally there are 14 stations, this configuration dates only from the eighteenth century. Many of the stations are legendary rather than scriptural, and it is a sad reflection on our prejudiced approach to the devotional customs of others that the churches of the Reformation didn't long ago devise their own set of stations limited to those incidents on the Lord's journey with undoubted scriptural warranty.

Historically the number of stations fluctuated wildly between 5 and 30, and today we should have no compunction in devising sets of stations of whatever number, provided they bring alive for us the stages of Christ's long lonely journey to his death.

One such attempt was that devised in 2005 in Philadelphia Cathedral using a set of photographs by local artist Jeannette Flamm, called 'Prayers at the Gate'. The photographs featured Ground Zero, and the adjoining St Paul's Chapel, in Manhattan, and Chimayo, a pilgrimage site in New Mexico. The images were displayed either singly or in groups around the cathedral to provide 14 stations by which our Lenten journey in the footsteps of Christ was made.

PRAYERS AT THE GATE are images from three distinct sites all of which exhibit the human need to set up shrines and create holy places when words are not enough. The images tell a story through the artefacts remaindered there by those who made pilgrimage: the baseball caps – and there are numerous ones – taken from visitors' heads and perched on the gates, which whisper 'From my head to your heart'; the handmade crosses and notes that are brought to, or created on, the site, express the prayer and communal longing for peace; the small dolls and fuzzy toys which, like the shawabti dolls of the native Americans, symbolize the caring for the souls of those mourned and our carrying them to eternity.

GROUND ZERO, NEW YORK

Since September 11, 2001 grief and prayer are being more openly expressed and made manifest in shrines of solace. America has been changing, reacting in new patterns.

Perhaps the need to share emotion is because of the violence erupting into our lives; prayer is not kept as a singularly private act or relegated only to traditional spaces or familiar patterns.

The site of the experience has become holy ground.

SANCTUARIO CHIMAYO, NEW MEXICO

The unprepossessing adobe chapel situated in the Chimayo Valley, New Mexico, lies between the Rio Grande and the Sangre de Cristo mountains. The rivers that water the valley rise in the snow-covered Truchas peaks and the Santa Cruz mountains and provide the valley with fertile soil to grow chili, fruit, beans, wheat and corn. The fruit and chilies are sold in the markets in Santa Fe – about one hour south.

The Chimayo area has long been considered blessed; moisture and high places were sacred to many of the Tewa and Pueblo Indians that have lived there for centuries.

The chapel was completed between 1814 and 1816. Because it was believed that the crucifix in the church miraculously moved itself, people came from afar to seek cures from earth taken from the chapel floor.

Today, visitors carry to the site hand-made crosses and crucifixes that they then bind to the fence at the edge of the chapel grounds. Many are also made at the site itself, using fallen cottonwood twigs and branches.

ST PAUL'S CHAPEL, NEW YORK

'What I think of most was all the love freely given to strangers by strangers.' (Ann Neary, Volunteer)

Following 9/11 persons came from all over the world to volunteer in the rescue effort for ground zero. And, children and adults from everywhere sent letters, poems, banners and personal items to St Paul's chapel in NY.

The chapel, the oldest public building in continuous use and the only remaining colonial era church in Manhattan, first opened in 1766. Situated adjacent to the site where the twin towers stood, the chapel became immediately after 9/11 a sanctuary for rescue workers, police officers and firefighters. They came to the chapel to eat and to rest and to pray. Some stretched out on pews to catch some sleep.

On September 14, 2001, with no electricity on site, the chapel's bells were rung by hand. The pastor, Fr Matthews, in a sermon on September 23 said, 'at times like this a bell becomes more than just a bell: it becomes a sacrament.'

Over the next nine months items were sent to St Paul's representing the compassion and love people felt for others – albeit complete strangers – in such a tragedy. The teddy bears sent by children were placed on the cots in the chapel for the volunteer workers, providing comfort and a touch of cheer.

St Paul's wrought iron fence became spontaneously a memorial site. Banners, poems, T-shirts, flags, letters, religious items, origami paper cranes signifying peace, were all placed there.

To witness these offerings was an inspiration.

And on the building facing the open pit the following words were painted: THE HUMAN SPIRIT IS NOT MEASURED BY THE SIZE OF THE ACT, BUT BY THE SIZE OF THE HEART.

Jeannette Flamm

In such circumstances as these, no wonder that an experience of the stations of the cross based on such painful realities, rather than on Veronica's cloth, grips our imaginations and takes holds of hearts and minds.

Sunday Liturgy

The penitential rite

This assumes a special significance during Lent, and time and trouble should be taken to ensure that this is no mere 'vain repetition' but an authentic and meaningful act of making our peace with God. Here we pause at the threshold of worship to petition a gracious God that, having 'squandered our inheritance in a distant country', we be allowed back at our father's table. We come in sorrow for all the ways we manage to make a mess of things, yet in hope, aware of God's endless mercy. We pray that broken relationships be restored and we be allowed to start all over again.

Music should play a key part in the penitential rite, for it unlocks our emotions and melts our stony hearts as nothing else can, but room must be found also for incisive words and for silence. Gesture too has a part to play, and in Lent it may be appropriate to incorporate tactile signs of mutual forgiveness and acceptance, such as turning to one's neighbour at the absolution and marking their forehead with the sign of the cross.

The baptismal font is a natural gathering place for the assembly in penitential mode, but the font being drained during Lent, we most likely remain in our places for the penitential rite. Alternatively the assembly may gather at the font anyway, water or no water, to be stopped dead in its tracks by this dried-up spring, this dry well. In this way our hunger for God 'as in a barren and dry land' (Psalm 63.1) can be heightened and given fresh poignancy.

In either case, silence should provide the liturgical punctuation by which this part of the liturgy is made quite distinct from the rest.

The communion

This is another point in the liturgy which in Lent can be treated differently to accentuate the season's special character. The precise formula is of secondary importance to the need to create an impact on our hearts and minds as we come to this moment of encounter with God. Because Lent is a time when we reflect on our track record as followers of Jesus of Nazareth, as disciples of his teaching and ambassadors of his ministry of reconciliation, it is a good time to use a method of sharing communion in which the assembly receives simultaneously.

One way of achieving this is to pass around the assembly a good number of baskets containing the broken bread, sufficient to ensure complete distribution without undue delay. Once every member of the assembly holds a piece of the consecrated bread, the presider announces the words of administration as the whole assembly consumes the sacrament at the same moment. The consecrated wine can then be distributed in a sufficient number of cups passed through the assembly, each person communicating his/her neighbour.

Lent setting

Palm Sunday: Eucharistic Prayer

Palm Sunday procession

Tasting the Passover food

Maundy Thursday

Good Friday

Altar of repose

The vigil

Easter Liturgy

Easter

Art for Eastertide Philadelphia 2008: 'Finding Surface' by Angela Victor

Banners at Kamloops Cathedral, British Columbia

The post-communion

Here the special character of the season can be marked, as was Advent, by a time of reflection following communion, when the members of the assembly disperse to find a quiet corner of the liturgical space. This time of reflection may be marked by total silence, or by silence as the setting for the spoken word, or music, to stand out in greater clarity as a focus of our thoughts.

Aftercare

The season of Lent provides a very good framework for Christian formation classes of various kinds, a tradition thoroughly in keeping with the ancient practice of using Lent as the final countdown period for the catechumens' preparation for initiation at the Easter Vigil. After the liturgy, therefore, coffee hour in Lent may usefully evolve into a simple bread and soup lunch, after which formation classes may be scheduled. This is particularly appropriate where the faith community comes from a wide area rather than a tight-knit neighbourhood, making it more attractive to use Sunday as a day for fellowship and learning as well as for worship.

See-at-a-glance Liturgy in Lent

Chair

Entrance – the Lent Prose in procession
Greeting
Penitential rite

Ambo

Prayer of the day
Reading from the Hebrew Scriptures
Psalm
Reading from the Christian Scriptures
Gospel acclamation
Gospel
Procession of the Gospel Book
Homily

Silence

Affirmation of faith
Prayers of the people

The Peace

Altar table

Song of offering
The eucharistic prayer
Sanctus
Lord's Prayer
Fraction
Communion

Reflection

Ambo

Post-communion prayer
Announcements
Sending out

Music for Sunday Liturgy in Lent

See Appendix 3 for full publishing details.

Entrance song

The Lent Prose (*Attende Domine*) sung in procession, plainchant, in *The Complete Celebration Hymnal*.

Penitential rite

Kyrie from Mass VIII, plainchant, in *Gregorian Missal*.

Psalm

'The Lord is my light and my salvation', David Haas, in *Ritual Song*.

Gospel acclamation

'Praise to you, O Christ our Saviour', Bernadette Farrell, in *Gather* and *The Complete Celebration Hymnal*.

Song of preparation of the table

'God's table', John Bell, in *Heaven Shall Not Wait*.

Song of offering

'Silent, surrendered', Margaret Rizza, in *Be Still and Know*.

Breaking of the bread

Agnus Dei from the Mass La Sérénité, Riyehee Hong, www.riyee.com

Communion song

'There is something holy here', Christopher Walker, OCP Publications (sheet music).

PASSIONTIDE

Traditionally covering the last two weeks of Lent, Passiontide is now for various reasons something of a liturgical white elephant.

Historical background

The fifth Sunday of Lent was by ancient custom known as Passion Sunday, and from the eleventh century it was the signal for all crosses, pictures and images to be veiled in purple cloth. On Good Friday the crucifix was unveiled as part of the devotions of that day. In the same period, the Gloria Patri was omitted from the recitation of the psalms, the introit and the Venite.

Characteristics

Among the reasons leading to the decline of Passiontide in the churches of the West is a natural desire to afford Holy Week a clear and distinct character as the forceful climax to the Lenten fast in immediate preparation for the great feast of Easter. A preceding week of medium severity inserted between Lent and Holy Week seems to blur the edges in a way which is unhelpful and unnecessary.

Furthermore, even for the most dedicated followers of tradition, the custom of the veiling of the crosses seemed to demand of the devout an ever greater ingenuity by way of explanation of meaning. It was one of those traditions the exact reasons for which seem to have been lost in the swirling mists of time. As a young curate I seemed to remember talk of the origin of veiling having something to do with hiding from the gaze of the faithful the bejewelled treasures of the sumptuous church interiors of past ages. This explanation, however, never seemed to carry much weight in an environment bedecked with the products of the ecclesiastical catalogue and second-hand liturgical bric-a-brac.

Cultural context

The death blow to Passiontide was, not surprisingly, the decision of the Roman Church in 1969 to put this mini-season out of its misery. As part of its liturgical tidying-up following Vatican II, Rome suppressed Passiontide, and transferred the name Passion Sunday from the fifth to the sixth Sunday of Lent.

The latter decision seems strangely unhelpful as a means of marking in the popular mind the beginning of the commemoration of Christ's last week of earthly pilgrimage. Everyone knows the story of the entry of Christ into Jerusalem on a day which for evermore would take its name from the branches the crowds tore from the near-by palm trees to bestrew his path. To rename the day by referencing an event yet to occur (even though we hear the account of the Passion liturgically on this day), seems rather contrary.

Common Worship (2000) refers to the old Passion Sunday as 'The Fifth Sunday of Lent', but indicates in small print beneath 'Passiontide begins'. This somewhat uneasy compromise is reflected in the collect for the day which, focusing on the cross of Christ, fails to chime with the readings provided by the Revised Common Lectionary, and suggests that the Church has not noticed that things have moved on.

By and large in the Western Church, even where Passion Sunday is no longer observed on the fifth Sunday in Lent, it is rarely transferred to displace Palm Sunday. The latter is too firmly entrenched in the popular mind to permit dethronement and makes admirable good sense in terms of pastoral theology. In most non-Roman churches, therefore, Palm Sunday continues to denote the Sunday inaugurating Holy Week. In company with Roman practice, however, 'Passiontide' is now in effect restricted to Holy Week, with no liturgical customs remaining to demarcate the penultimate week of Lent as a special time distinct from the rest of the Lenten fast which precedes it.

6 HOLY WEEK

Holy Week is really a season within a season; an intense final week of the Lenten fast in which the final days in the life and ministry of Jesus of Nazareth are played out in the reality of the present moment.

Historical background

Originally, the memorial of the death and resurrection of the Christ followed a weekly, as opposed to an annual, pattern, for every Sunday was a new beginning, a fresh 'First Day' energized by the presence of the Risen Lord among the people gathered in his name.

As part of a gradual and inevitable process, at a date now impossible to determine, the early Christian communities expressed their desire to honour their Lord in an annual observance of these saving events. The name given to this annual commemoration was *Pascha* – derived from *pesach*, the Hebrew word for 'Passover'. For the first three centuries the *Pascha* was a night-long vigil culminating in a celebration of the eucharist as dawn broke. This followed a fast in preparation for Easter which, although consisting of merely two or three days as opposed to forty, was no doubt a real one, with no tea breaks.

Later, probably during the fourth century, and growing out of the increasing popularity of making pilgrimage to Jerusalem to re-enact the last days in the life of Jesus, this simple *Pascha* evolved into the fully fledged re-enactment of all the dramatic events crowded into the Lord's final days. This pattern of ritual observances was regularized and shaped into the package of liturgical events we now know as Holy Week.

This enabled every Christian community, however far from Jerusalem it might be, to be present through liturgical observance at all the events that befell Jesus of Nazareth in his last days. This included his triumphant entrance into the capital, his confrontation with the religious authorities, his final meal with his inner circle, to his betrayal, arrest and execution, and finally his vindication and triumph.

Between Palm Sunday and Easter morning, the Christian was enabled to enter into the mystery of Christ's suffering, death and resurrection and make it his/her own. Long before the mass media was even thought of, Holy Week was a triumph in the communication of ideas in a dramatic way which could take hold of people's lives and change them for ever.

Characteristics

Holy Week does not of course involve the remembering, the reliving, of past events which must remain for ever lost to us. Just as the celebration of the eucharist is a great deal more than the remembrance of the Last Supper, but is also, and more importantly, a participation in a sacred meal with the Risen Lord and a foretaste of the heavenly banquet, so Holy Week is present encounter as much as past recollection.

No matter how dreadful the events that we commemorate in the last days of Jesus, we know the end of the movie; it is Christ Risen and glorified who bids us take up our cross to follow him. Furthermore we follow not only in re-enactment, but in re-energized discipleship, as agents of transformation – of ourselves and of a direction-less and hungry world.

Entering into the mysteries which Holy Week holds for us can be a life-changing experience, and it is pre-eminently the time and place in the Church's Year where liturgy as conversion experience is most frequently encountered. It is best approached therefore as a supremely important moment in our journey as a community of faith, so that no one is left with the impression that it is some sort of optional extra appealing only to the church nerd.

Holy Week is an 'all hands on deck' event, when all leave is cancelled and all bets are off. Weeks, even months, ahead, the faith community needs to be reminded of the dates of the crucial events of Holy Week, and urged to reorganize well ahead of time their personal diaries around these sacred days.

Cultural context

That being said, the frantic pace of contemporary Western culture has in many areas pressured Christian communities into a 'Sundays only' ritual observance, as instanced by the frequent transfer of many major festivals – most notably Epiphany and Ascension – to the nearest Sunday. We can safely say therefore that the concept of hoisting the average congregation out of the morass of secular daily routines to gather for worship every single day of Holy Week takes on an air of unreality.

Although the Monday, Tuesday and Wednesday of Holy Week are likely to remain an acquired taste for busy Christians, we can however make the maximum liturgical capital out of Palm Sunday and the Triduum itself. These sacred Three Days cover Maundy Thursday, Good Friday and Holy Saturday, although nowadays the 'liturgy' of the last of these is likely to consist of a marathon of preparation, decoration and fire-laying, albeit prefaced by an attenuated Morning Prayer.

If there ever comes a day when we transfer Maundy Thursday and Good Friday to the nearest Sunday, to celebrate some sort of 'Omnibus Edition' of Holy Week and Easter in one go, then we shall know it's time for the Christian Church to shut up shop.

PALM SUNDAY

Palm Sunday: the procession to the place of assembly

Characteristics

Two liturgical events dominate this day: the re-enactment of Jesus' entry into Jerusalem, and the reading of the Passion narrative. These two events each claim this Sunday as their own, resulting in some degree of confusion as to its character and nomenclature. 'Palm Sunday' is the designation used here, not just because this title is retained in *Common Worship* (2000), but also because the entry into Jerusalem is what dominates the thoughts of the average worshipper on this day, a fact of life which serves very well our pastoral purpose of inaugurating a week-long series of liturgical commemorations. Today we enter with Christ into a showdown situation; as his followers, our bluff is to be called, and in the coming days we will see what we are made of.

Choreography

If therefore the theme of entry is to be made primary, we must allow no obstacle to prevent the incorporation into our Palm Sunday Liturgy of a real journey, an actual movement from a gathering place to a place of engagement. In many cases it makes good sense to first gather the assembly in the church hall or school or other building where we can conveniently assemble. This solution provides insurance against bad weather, but for the brave-hearted a venue out of doors can also be effective, and what we may lose in audibility and crispness of liturgical action will be more than compensated for in the high visibility gained by which the assembly of faith can give witness to the wider community of its primary work of worship and prayer.

Even more effective in terms of public witness is the choice of a venue for the opening of the liturgy in a building or open space at some distance from the church building, even at the other end of the parish. At St Jude's, Peterborough, the blessing of palms often took place in a local authority school at one end of the parish, from which venue the Palm Sunday procession would wend its way to the parish church at the other end. This certainly made an impact, and even the occasional catcall added a certain authenticity to our attempts to follow in the footsteps of Christ through these sacred days. In passing, we note that worshippers in the New World face no such problems when organizing outdoor worship (though the enemy within is always the more dangerous).

In planning our Palm Sunday procession, it is worth pausing to consider all the options. We nearly always imagine a Palm Sunday procession taking this course; from outside to inside, from away to home, from unknown to known. By contrast, the journey of Christ on this day was the culmination of his 'going up to Jerusalem' to face betrayal, humiliation and almost certain death. Although for Jesus, as for any Jew, Jerusalem was his spiritual home, his pilgrimage destination, it nevertheless involved him in a journey from security into danger. From his Galilee power base he ventured into the volatile uncertainty of his volatile capital city – a powder-keg, then as now.

It would be instructive therefore in terms of pastoral theology to reverse the order, at least in some years, and to travel on this day from the security of the parish church to the unknown quantity of the function room of a pub at the other end of the parish, perhaps even on the wrong side of the tracks. The possibilities are endless, but any of them may help jerk us out of a Holy Week experience which is demanding in time commitment only, merely reaffirming and reassuring us in the familiar and predictable. We need some element in every Holy Week that recalls us to an experience of following Jesus to a life at the edge. Something to discomfort us will be no bad thing.

Wherever we choose to assemble for the blessing of palms, there are but a few basic requirements: a simple table with a white cloth, a room nearby where the liturgical ministers can vest, and sufficient space for the assembly to gather around. Palms should be distributed to the assembly as people arrive, so that everyone will be ready to hold up palms for the blessing.

Following a suitable 'call to order' – a roll on the drums, a trumpet sound – the president greets the people and introduces the rite that follows in the context of our Lenten journey. The introduction found on page 270 of *Common Worship: Times and Seasons* (2006), and the blessing that follows, serve the purpose very well. The palms are blessed, preferably with holy water and incense as well as words, and the palm Gospel (that is, the Gospel passage recording the event now being re-enacted) is proclaimed.

The procession is then formed, led by the thurifer and acolytes carrying enclosed lanterns (as opposed to unprotected candles which require constant relighting and give rise to unnecessary increases in blood pressure), with the president and other ministers bringing up the rear. Where there is no thurifer, a crucifer should lead the procession, accompanied by the acolytes.

Congregational singing in outdoor processions should be avoided. It inevitably becomes so ragged and unsynchronized that the end result is the kind of witness you want to keep quiet about. Far better to use percussion to give a steady beat, or brass to play hymns as instrumentals, even if this means hiring a professional or two. It is well worth the investment to be able to launch so important an event in our annual pilgrimage with dignity and panache.

As the procession enters the space where the eucharist is to be celebrated, a suitable hymn is taken up with growing intensity as the crowd swells. This may be the traditional 'All glory, laud and honour', or the more contemporary 'Make way, make way, for Christ our King', or some other suitable song of acclamation, as the assembly enters with joy its own 'Jerusalem'.

Once we reach the place of eucharistic assembly, whether in a familiar or unusual location, the eucharistic rite continues as normal with the opening prayer of the day, the preparation and procession rendering a penitential rite unnecessary. Following the second reading, we get ready for the solemn reading of the Passion narrative. Although a Gospel reading, it is not announced or acclaimed in the usual way, and may need no musical preface of any kind, except that it is often useful to cover the movement of the readers into their positions. For this, perhaps the singing of a single refrain from the Gospel acclamation we have used in Lent may suffice.

Palm Sunday: the eucharistic assembly

The reading of the Passion provides an excellent opportunity for getting creative in the liturgical use of the Scriptures. A whole group of readers should be recruited, and great attention given to maximizing the impact of the narrative on the assembly. The readers need to be clearly heard, with or without microphones as circumstances dictate, and this will require more than turning up on the day and hoping for the best. Good training and intensive rehearsal is needed to make the most of this moment. The dramatic impact of the Passion can be further heightened by dispersing readers around the building, especially where there is a gallery or transept from which dis-embodied voices can sound forth.

If the assembly is going to be encouraged to listen and take it in, they need to be seated, but asked to stand at the description of the death of Jesus, and then to remain standing to the end. The length of the passage used should be given careful consideration to arrive at what is a reasonable length to retain the attention of the listener while nevertheless flagging up this reading as something very different indeed from the regular Sunday Gospel. *Common Worship* (2000) provides for each year of the three-year cycle a shortened version of the Passion narrative which contains the essential section of the trial and execution, and these versions are nearly always to be preferred.

The Passion ends without announcement or acclamation, and the assembly sits. In many ways, silence is the only adequate response to what has been heard, but the president or another minister may wish to add a brief comment drawing out the significance of what the assembly is engaged in doing. The dual nature of the day demands a lot of the preacher. When the Passion narrative is paramount, futher comment is largely unnecessary. Where the Entry into Jerusalem dominates, there is more scope for a homily. In either case, restraint is the order of the day.

Following an appropriate period of silence after the Passion or accompanying commentary or homily, the remainder of the eucharistic liturgy continues as normal.

MONDAY, TUESDAY AND WEDNESDAY IN HOLY WEEK

Common Worship (2000) provides special readings for Monday, Tuesday and Wednesday in Holy Week (though not a special collect for each day, unlike the Episcopal Church), and these days should of course be observed with care and devotion, with their wider observance quietly encouraged.

Although these days provide the faithful with a very particular experience of quiet preparation with our Lord, they are not likely to involve large numbers. Indeed, the comparatively smaller numbers contribute part of their appeal. These are days for the closest disciples to be 'taken aside' by their Teacher with words for their ears alone as the storm clouds gather and darken.

THE THREE DAYS

The Three Days ('*Triduum Sacrum*') is the name given to the sacred three days of Maundy Thursday, Good Friday and Holy Saturday, immediately prior to Easter, commemorating the final meal, the betrayal and arrest, and the trial, execution and burial of Jesus the Christ.

MAUNDY THURSDAY

The Thursday of Holy Week is, liturgically speaking, one crazy mixed-up kid, with lots of things going on inside its head. As far as the worshipper at the local church is concerned, however, the matter is relatively straightforward.

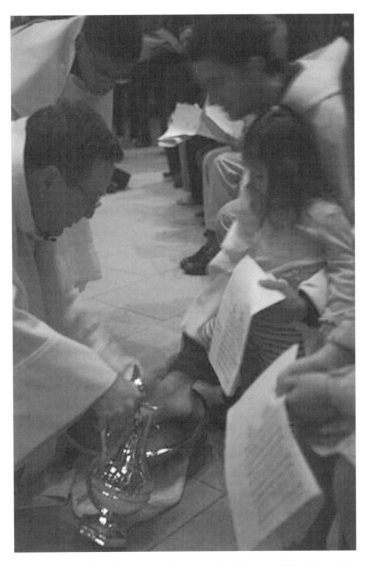

Maundy Thursday: foot-washing at the Mass of the Last Supper

Historical background

Historically, this day has hosted three distinct liturgical celebrations. The oldest of these was to do with the public reconciliation of penitents prior to their readmission to communion at Easter. We can safely say that in today's world this would fly like a lead balloon, and it is small wonder that this liturgy fell into disuse many centuries ago.

Characteristics

Two liturgical celebrations associated with this day survive and flourish:

- **Chrism Mass.** The diocesan rite of the Chrism Mass is celebrated by the bishop in his (or her) cathedral, or other major church, at which the oil for the ministries involving anointing is blessed for the coming year. To this was added, following Vatican II, the renewal of ordination vows for all diocesan clergy, and this has been widely adopted by dioceses in the Anglican Communion also. Although the Chrism Mass will always include some lay participants, it can be said to be by and large 'trade only'. This is a pity, as it can be an inspiring celebration of the communal life of a diocese and of the priestly life of those set apart for service in ordination.
- **Mass of the Last Supper.** The rite that defines this day as far as the vast majority of church members is concerned is the annual commemoration of the events surrounding the last meal that Jesus shared with his immediate circle, only hours before his arrest. According to the three Synoptic Gospels, this was clearly a Passover meal, arranged by Jesus with meticulous intentionality. By the time the day was over (that is, before sunset on the Friday), his life had been offered up.

Cultural context

It is a pity that the meaning of Maundy Thursday has become somewhat obscured, in England at least, by the custom of the monarch distributing token gifts (the Royal Maundy) to senior citizens on this day. The origin of the name is far more interesting and significant, coming from the Latin word for commandment (*mandatum*) used in the ancient antiphon for this day from John 13.34: 'I give you a new commandment, that you love one another.' Despite Rome's preference for 'Holy Thursday', the name

Maundy Thursday is a good one full of meaning and we should reclaim and restore it to its full liturgical significance.

Components

The Chrism Eucharist

For those ordained to ministry in the Church, Maundy Thursday continues to mean, in addition to the evening Mass of the Last Supper, their gathering with their bishop in the mother church of the diocese for the morning Chrism Eucharist. Full provision for this is included in *Common Worship: Times and Seasons* (2006, p. 278), together with a useful historical note. At this eucharist, the oils to be used in the Church's ministry of anointing, as enjoined by the Letter of James 5.15, are blessed by the bishop and distributed to the clergy present to be taken for use in the parishes of the diocese.

Taking a leaf out of the Roman book, in a practice introduced by Pope Paul VI in the late 1960s, a further dimension is often added in which the bishop invites the priests present to reaffirm their ordination vows. This is often broadened to include deacons, readers and other authorized ministers. Although this ultimately only makes sense within the context of the common call of all God's people to ministry by virtue of their baptism, the renewal of commitment to ministry at the Chrism Eucharist pertains only to particular ministries of a public nature. It is a bonding exercise between those set apart for the ministry of the Church, a calling which can involve isolation and misunderstanding as well as privilege and status. It can be a deeply moving ceremony made all the more significant amidst the contemporary temptations to mistrust and polarization.

The renewal of commitment by the whole people of God is properly emphasized at the Easter Vigil at the rites of Christian initiation. Although not forming part of the Chrism Eucharist in the English rite as set out in *Common Worship: Times and Seasons* (2006), the foot-washing may also be included in this diocesan liturgy. Here the bishop(s) of the diocese wash the feet of their clergy to model in themselves Christ's own pattern of servant ministry. In today's ecclesiastical climate, the acceptance by the recipients can be as significant as the offer of service on the part of the minister.

The stage management of the Chrism Mass is usually the responsibility of a cathedral or other large church where a staff team is available to swing into action. It therefore remains beyond the scope of a work dealing primarily with worship in the local church. Suffice it to say that the Chrism Mass is an occasion in the life of a diocese of tremendous importance in building mutual trust and loyalty, one when great attention to detail is required to create a liturgy memorable for its noble simplicity and understated solemnity, produced by an outfit one is proud to belong to. It comes at an interesting point in the journey through Lent and Holy Week: the troops are coming up to the final push but can see light at the end of the tunnel. They are serious-minded, but capable of becoming de-mob happy at the drop of a hat. After all, they know the end of the movie.

The Eucharist of the Last Supper

Although all members of the Church should make the effort to witness at least once in their lives that powerful reaffirmation of those called to call forth and foster the ministry of others, for the vast majority of Christians Maundy Thursday will continue to mean the evening commemoration of the final meal of Jesus with his friends. Here among his inner circle, one of whom was a traitor, he made his last farewells and went out into the night to wrestle with God and to face death.

Maundy Thursday night is really the heart of Holy Week, the pivotal moment in which the die is cast and from which all else follows. This evening celebration really marks the beginning of the Triduum. In the framework of these last days of Jesus, it is the wrestling within himself which is the true battleground. His subsequent execution, though horrendous, is but the inevitable consequence of the decision wrung from him alone in the garden, his dreams shattered by desertion and betrayal.

Maundy Thursday is therefore the supreme example in the Church's Year of liturgy as *formation*. It is the night when disciples are made or broken. Indeed, to describe the whole process of Jesus' 'going up to Jerusalem' we could do no better than borrow the haunting and evocative title of Eugene O'Neill's play *A Long Day's Journey into Night*.

Setting

To enter appropriately into the mystery of this night, a community of faith needs to take a fresh look at the various spaces available to it (perhaps some it has never thought of using before), and boldly and imaginatively create two distinct theatres of worship: a 'large room upstairs, furnished and ready' (Mark 14.15), and at a little distance 'a place called Gethsemane' (Mark 14.32).

It is not often that we will be able to honour the 'upstairs' angle of the story, but it is certainly possible to go to town on transforming our regular worship space into an

*Maundy Thursday: a liturgical space transformed
into an 'upper room'*

intimate dining-room. For once we should forget the formal altar table and instead, using any old tables we can lay our hands on, cobble together one long table covered in white cloths stretching down the liturgical space, around which the 'disciples' of our own generation may sit.

We should allow those in our assembly gifted in interior or theatre design full rein with drapes and special lighting to totally change the character of the space. Preparation of the liturgical space for Maundy Thursday (as for Easter morning) will mean some overtime for that all-age planning and preparation group on perhaps several Saturdays in Lent.

Nightlights on the table may be all the lighting needed (lit ceremonially as part of the liturgy), provided that those leading the liturgy have sufficient supplementary lighting for their particular tasks.

This is not so much to create the illusion of a Palestinian interior of the period, but to produce a dramatic impact upon the sensibilities of the assembly, making the point that here they have stumbled onto something completely different. This is not just a question of 'same time, same place' with a few special readings and visual aids, but the liturgical scene of a showdown. The space and the occasion demand a response. Who is there here who will walk with the US Marshall down Main Street to call the bad guys out of the saloon? This is the time to choose, and it could well be a life-or-death decision.

It is worth interjecting here that if attempting such a reconfiguration of the space is rendered impossible by an immovable phalanx of pews, then the greater our frustration at the way in which fixed furniture of this type renders a church building unusable for creative liturgy, and the speedier our faculty petition for the pews' removal.

Unless numbers are small, it is unlikely that it will be possible to seat every member of the assembly directly *at* the table, but in any case it is preferable that all should be seated a little back from it, to allow movement at various stages of the liturgy.

Cultural context

Wherever we find ourselves amidst the debate among New Testament scholars as to the nature of Jesus' last meal – Passover or preparation – it remains indisputably an occasion grounded in Jewish ritual and Jewish hopes and expectations. Because we know the end of the movie, there is for the Christian community more to it than that, but the starting point remains a Jewish Seder or Passover meal, on which are overlaid several layers of Christian meaning and significance. These layers embrace both looking back to the Last Supper, the present reality of the Risen Christ in the breaking of the bread, and the future expectation of the heavenly banquet.

The starting point of our liturgy therefore presents us with an ideal opportunity to celebrate the common roots of journeying faith with the Jewish tradition from which we emerged. This becomes highly desirable when we consider the shameful history of Christian discrimination and violence against Jews, the religious tradition which (despite its being Jesus' own) we have conveniently recast in the role of deicidal scapegoat.

Every leader of Christian worship should make it his/her business to become familiar with the basic outline of a Jewish Seder, not only in book theory, but in the practice of faith communities of our day and in one's neighbourhood. Attendance at a Seder in a Jewish household can be a powerful experience of how an age-old story of seeking God is reborn and relived in the immediate and the here and now, in the simple and always accessible context of friends around a table sharing food and wine.

Christians have a great deal to learn here about devout worship celebrated in simple rituals in a domestic setting. The Seder is a very inter-generational occasion, and traditionally it is the youngest person present who, in accordance with Exodus 12.26, asks the question of those gathered round the table, 'What do you mean by this observance?' This presents us with a simple yet powerful means of preserving, with each succeeding generation, an ancient faith story.

The asking of the four questions is the cue for the elders to go to town, extolling God's praises, not just for the original Passover and Exodus but for all subsequent blessings, not least on all those present at this particular Seder. It is a night for recounting and storytelling, for learning Torah and for sharing good things, and may go on well into the night, even into the early hours of the next morning.

Music also plays an important part in the festivities, and as well as traditional Passover songs may include songs of liberation from all over the world, including freedom songs from South Africa, or spirituals from North America. For example, the well-known spiritual 'Let my people go' is a song that everyone can easily join in, Jews and non-Jews alike.

The Seder

The Passover Seder is a ritual feast taking place on the first evening of the Jewish holiday of Passover which commemorates the rescue of the children of Israel from enslavement in Egypt and their safe passage across the Red Sea.

The text of the story framing the rituals of this night is called the Haggadah,[1] and it is the hope of the faithful Jew in reciting it to 'articulate the prayer that is in the heart of every Jew, the prayer for a world which will be rid of all Pharaohs, and in which God alone will be sovereign'.[2]

The context of the Seder is the domestic household, not the synagogue, where family and friends gather round a communal table on which is set out food of highly symbolic meaning consumed in a highly ritualistic way.

The Jewish experience of the Seder is the precursor of the way in which the Christian experiences Holy Week. It is past event made present reality: '*Pesah* is not merely the commemoration of an important event in our past but an event in which *we* participated and in which we continue to participate. It is our own story, not just some ancient history that we retell.'[3]

It could be said indeed that the Jew has an even stronger sense of participation in the Passover than the Christian in the *pasch* of Christ, because it is through blood relationship as well as religious heritage. Jews can say 'we participated' in the Passover, in a way which the Christian cannot pretend to have participated in the *pasch* of the Lord, even though we participate in it now. This is but one of the many reasons why our Jewish brothers and sisters have so much to teach us.

We talk easily enough of 'apostolic succession' in relation to ordained ministries, but in the Judaic tradition there is a deep and powerful sense of spiritual succession for each and every Jew. 'To continue our 3,000 year history, each of us and each of our children must feel as though we ourselves were slaves in Egypt and were redeemed. In this way, each new generation can take its place in the chain of the Jewish people leading down from the Exodus to the present.'[4] Oh that Christians could say half as much about their sense of engagement in the events of the first Holy Week two thousand years ago.

Significantly, children play a primary role in the Seder ritual, an aspect where again the Jewish tradition has much to teach the Christian. In the Haggadah contained in *A Night of Questions,* four children are given voice at the table – symbolically one wise, one wicked, one simple, and one who does not know how to ask – reflecting the four aspects of every personality.

Furthermore, an additional cup – the cup of Miriam, containing spring water – is placed prominently on the table, and sipped from throughout the meal. This cup represents the important voice of Miriam and of all women in the story of the Exodus, righting the wrongs of many centuries.

The centrepiece of the table is a large Seder plate on which are arranged the traditional foods, each of them symbolic, which carry the story forward:

Karpas – a green vegetable or herb such as parsley, symbolizing spring and rebirth, which is dipped in salt water near the beginning of the meal.

Haroset – a mixture of chopped apples, nuts and spices, and sometimes raisins, dates or figs, mingled with wine or grape juice. This mixture symbolizes the mortar used by the slaves in Egypt to lay their bricks, its sweetness offsetting the taste of the bitter herbs.

Maror – the bitter herbs, usually horseradish or romaine lettuce, symbolizing the bitterness of slavery.

Beytzah – hard-boiled egg, which is then, still in its shell, roasted in the oven until part of it is scorched. The egg symbolizes the festival sacrifice.

Zeroa – roasted shank bone of lamb, symbol of the Passover lamb. In some Jewish communities, grilled beet is allowed as a vegetarian substitute.

Also on the table are arranged:

Matzot – three matzot, one on top of the other, are placed next to the Seder plate and covered with a napkin or special cloth.

Wine or grape juice – four cups of wine are drunk during the Seder. Depending on the age and preference of those taking part, a ritual tasting may be more appropriate than large consumption, and grape juice can be substituted. Growing sleepy or tipsy at the Seder is not the name of the game.

Salt water – bowls of salt water are placed on the table, representing the tears of slavery.

Two large cups or goblets – these are placed prominently on the table:

> *Miriam's cup*, filled with spring water, representing the well of Miriam that sustained the Israelites in the wilderness
>
> *Elijah's cup* – placed ready for Elijah, who will usher in the messianic days of deliverance.

The Seder traditionally begins as darkness falls, and is accompanied by a ritual lighting of candles, as this prayer is recited:

> Blessed are you, Eternal One our God, sovereign of all worlds, who has made us holy with your mitzvot and commanded us to kindle the lights.

The Seder then begins, and contains a succession of ritualistic actions and recited texts, each of which bears witness to an aspect of the story of the Passover. Essential components of the Seder are:

- blessing of wine (*kadesh*)
- washing of hands (*urehatz*)
- dipping the green vegetable in salt water (*karpas*)
- breaking the middle matzah (*yahatz*)
- telling the story (*magi*). The story is retold in response to four questions asked by the youngest child present, reliving the dialogue set out in Exodus 12.26, which opens with 'And when your children ask you, "What do you mean by this observance?" The prescribed response is the telling of the story of the first Passover: the 'passing over' by the Lord of the households of the Israelites, the doorways of whose houses had been daubed with the blood of slain lambs to distinguish them from those of the rest of the population.
- hand-washing (*rohtzah*)
- eating matzah (*motzi matzah*)
- eating bitter herbs (*maror*)
- eating matzah and maror sandwich (*koreh*)
- the meal (*shulnan oreh*)
- eating the afikoman (the portion of the middle matzah, hidden at the beginning of the Seder)
- blessings after the meal (*bareh*)

- reciting psalms (*hallel*)
- conclusion (*nirtzah*)

Interspersed throughout the meal is the drinking of four cups of wine at various points, culminating in the ceremony of the cup of Elijah, when each pours a little wine into Elijah's cup, and the company stands as the door of the room is opened for Elijah to enter.

With thanks to Carl and Pecki Witonski of Lower Merion, Pennsylvania, whose gift for hospitality makes possible in their home a Seder incorporating many faith traditions.

Choreography

One way in which the experience of the Seder may be applied to our own liturgy on Maundy Thursday night is for us to use a continuous narrative weaving together into one whole the three separate readings from Exodus, First Corinthians and John given us in the Lectionary.

But the ministers of the liturgy must first enter the room, and getting this right on Maundy Thursday is a tricky thing. The mood of this liturgy is reflective and restrained, and deeply poignant. Although we know the end of the movie, nevertheless any hint of triumphalism would be out of place. For this reason, an appropriate beginning in keeping with this mood would be for the ministers to be already seated as people arrive, and for silence to be maintained. This may, however, present a problem in starting the liturgy in a simple yet significant fashion.

Alternatively, the ministers and the whole of the assembly might enter together, walking informally rather than processing, from another gathering space, into the eucharistic room, as one might proceed at a formal dinner from a reception area into the dining-room itself. This, however, might strike a false note of special celebration on so solemn a night. Most likely the solution will be for the assembly to gather quietly in the place where the meal is to be shared, after which the liturgical ministers enter without undue ceremony, during a carefully chosen entrance song that sets the tone.

Once all have assembled, the president greets the assembly and invites some of the younger members of the assembly to light with tapers the lamps on the tables, as a suitable song is sung. The simple chant, 'Kindle a flame, to lighten the dark, and take our fear away', by John Bell (1998) would work very well.

The president next says the prayer of the day, and then asks the assembly to be seated as he/she introduces the liturgy. Nothing more is needed by way of a homily,

Mass of the Last Supper: tasting the food of Passover

for on this night above all others the liturgy speaks for itself, and a preacher's words inevitably seem intrusive and superfluous.

The continuous narrative rearranges the three traditional readings, placing the section from John's Gospel before that from Paul's letter to Corinth, in order to maintain the sequence of events in a sensible chronological order, the foot-washing thereby coming before the account of Jesus' blessing of bread and wine as a prefiguring of his own fate the next day. Various versions of the text, which include frequent acclamations for the assembly, are in circulation (see p. 107), and if none are to be found it is a comparatively easy task to go the Scriptures and quarry them for yourself.

A group of well-trained readers, including four children, will be required, who have set aside time to rehearse together. The readers then group themselves around the ambo or disperse themselves throughout the assembly, as preferred. Once the president has introduced the liturgy, the readers begin their narrative with the Exodus account of the first Passover, using as many voices as are necessary to play the several different roles involved. The children's voices will be particularly effective in the reading of the question 'What do you mean by this observance?' (Exodus 12.26) in accordance with Hebrew tradition.

This section of the narrative can be enlivened with music from various sources on the theme of liberation from slavery, of which the Negro spiritual tradition is one notable example.

At the appropriate moment in the reading from Exodus, a pause is made in the narrative, and assistants who have previously prepared samples of the food specified in the Exodus account – unleavened bread, bitter herbs and roast lamb (Exodus 12.8) – bring them forward to place on the table. Today any local supermarket will supply matzos for unleavened bread and coarse horseradish for the bitter herbs to garnish the lamb, which is cut up into tiny strips. The president invites the assembly to come forward and to eat, standing and in silence, this taste of the food of our spiritual ancestors. We eat it at the ready, prepared for action, eager to move, for 'this is how you shall eat it: your loins girded, your sandals on your feet, and your staff in your hand; and you shall eat it hurriedly. It is the passover of the Lord' (Exodus 12.11). This is no relaxed meal, but a quick bite before a perilous journey.

Once everyone has tasted the food, people return to their places and the narrative continues, punctuated by acclamations proclaimed by the narrator and repeated by the whole assembly, and by music as and when required.

The narrative then moves seamlessly from the Exodus account of the institution of the Passover into the gospel account of the meal celebrated by Jesus himself at his last Passover and on his last night. Of particular significance is the Fourth Gospel's account of Jesus' new commandment (*mandatum*) to love, from which this day takes its name, and the institution of servant leadership enshrined in the washing of the disciples' feet.

Maundy Thursday:
The Mass of the Last Supper

The Scripture readings – combined form

Narrator: While the Israelites were still in bondage in the land of Egypt, the Lord spoke to Moses and his brother, Aaron:

Reader 1: You must speak to the entire community of Israel and say

Reader 2: On the tenth of this month, each household must take and slaughter a lamb without blemish. You must put some of the blood on the doorposts and lintels of your houses. That night, the lamb is to be eaten roasted over the fire. You must not have anything left over; whatever is not eaten must be burned.

Reader 3: You shall eat it standing up, with your shoes and coats on, and with your staff in your hand. You must eat it quickly.

Reader 1: This is a Passover in honour of the Lord.

Reader 2: On that night I am going to go through the whole land of Egypt and strike down every firstborn in the land, man and beast alike.

Reader 3: The blood of the lamb will serve to mark the houses where you live. When I see the blood, I will pass over you and you will escape the destruction.

Narrator:
Blessed are you!
Blessed are you!
Blessed are you, O Lord our God.
Blessed are you, O Lord our God.
Blessed are you, O Lord our God, who spared our ancestors in faith.
Blessed are you, O Lord our God, who spared our ancestors in faith.

The assembly sings: 'Bless the Lord, my soul' (Taizé)

Narrator: The Lord also told his people,

Reader 1: From now on you are to celebrate this Passover as a feast in honour of the Lord.

Reader 2: It is to be kept as a day of festival for all generations to come.

Reader 3: You are to celebrate it for ever.

Narrator:
Blessed are you!
Blessed are you!
Blessed are you, O Lord our God.
Blessed are you, O Lord our God.
Blessed are you, O Lord our God, who has given us this feast.
Blessed are you, O Lord our God, who has given us this feast.

The assembly repeats: 'Bless the Lord, my soul' (Taizé)

Narrator: And so Moses summoned all the elders of Israel, and told them everything that the Lord had commanded him to say.

Reader 1: When the Israelites heard the message, they bowed down and worshipped the Lord. Then they hurried back to their homes and did all that the Lord had commanded.

Reader 2: And it came to pass that the angel of the Lord struck down the firstborn of all the land of Egypt, man and beast alike.

Reader 3: But when the angel found a house with blood on the lintel and door posts, he passed over and spared those inside.

Narrator:

Blessed be God!

Blessed be God!

Blessed be God in his mercy.

Blessed be God in his mercy.

Blessed be God in his mercy, holy his name.

Blessed be God in his mercy, holy his name.

The assembly repeats: 'Bless the Lord, my soul' (Taizé)

At this point the traditional Passover food is brought forward and placed on the tables.

Narrator: And so each year the people of God celebrated this feast in his honour. Parents explained its meaning to their children, and they in turn explained it to their children.

First child: Why is this night different from all other nights?

Second child: Why on this night do we eat only unleavened bread?

Third child: Why on this night do we eat bitter herbs?

Fourth child: Why do we eat standing up?

Narrator: We do these things in honour of the Passover of the Lord.

Reader 1: Once, we were slaves in the land of Egypt, but the Lord rescued us on this holy night. That is why this night is for ever special, and different from all other nights.

Reader 2: We eat unleavened bread because there was no time that night to let it rise.

Reader 3: We eat bitter herbs to remind us of the bitterness of slavery.

Reader 1: We eat standing up because our ancestors were ready to go that night, without a moment's delay.

Narrator: For thirteen hundred years our ancestors celebrated the Passover. And at the end of that time, Jesus, God's Anointed One, came to celebrate it on his last night with his friends. He left it, and us, changed for ever.

Here the presider invites members of the assembly to come forward and, standing at the table, share the food. After the members of the assembly have returned to their places, the following acclamation is said:

Narrator:
Blessed be God!
Blessed be God!
Blessed be God in Jesus, his Anointed One.
Blessed be God in Jesus, his Anointed One.
Blessed be God in Jesus, his Anointed One, our new Passover lamb.
Blessed be God in Jesus, his Anointed One, our new Passover lamb.

(The assembly sings: 'Will you let me be your servant?' (Gillard)

Narrator: On the night before he died, Jesus celebrated the Passover for the last time with his disciples. He knew the end had come. He had always loved those who were his, but now he showed how perfect his love was.

Reader 1: They were all seated at supper. Judas had already yielded to the temptation to betray Jesus as soon as opportunity arose. Jesus knew that he came from God and was going back to God, and that the Father had put everything in his hands.

Reader 2: He got up from the table, removed his outer garment and tied a towel around his waist. Then he poured water into a basin and began to wash the disciples' feet, and to wipe them dry with the towel around his waist.

Narrator: He came to Simon Peter, who asked him,

Reader 1: Lord, are you going to wash my feet?

Narrator: Jesus answered,

Reader 2: I know you don't understand what I'm doing now, but later you will.

Narrator: Peter exclaimed,

Reader 1: Never! You shall never wash my feet!

Narrator: Jesus answered Peter,

Reader 2: If I do not wash you, you can share nothing with me.

Narrator: Peter relented and said,

Reader 1: Then wash my hands and face as well!

Narrator: Hearing this, Jesus commented,

Reader 2: No one who has taken a bath needs to wash again; he is clean all over.

Narrator:
Blessed be God!

Blessed be God!
Blessed be God in Jesus, his Anointed.
Blessed be God in Jesus, his Anointed.
Blessed be God in Jesus, his Anointed, who washes us clean.
Blessed be God in Jesus, his Anointed, who washes us clean.

The presiding minister and others wash the feet of the members of the assembly.

The assembly sings: 'Drop, drop slow tears'
'My song is love unknown'

Choral reflection: 'God so loved the world' (Stainer)

Narrator: When he had finished washing their feet, he put on his clothes again and sat down. He asked them,

Reader 1: Do you understand what I have done to you? You call me master and Lord, and that is what I am. Well, if I, your master and Lord, have washed your feet, then you should wash each other's feet.

Narrator:
Blessed be God!
Blessed be God!
Blessed be God in Jesus, who washes us clean.
Blessed be God in Jesus, who washes us clean.

Narrator: Then Jesus took bread, and gave thanks for it:

Reader 3: Blessed are you, O Lord our God, King of the universe, who has brought forth bread from the earth.

Narrator: He broke the bread and gave it to his disciples, saying,

Reader 3: This is my body, which will be broken for you. Do this, to remember me.

Narrator: Then he took the cup of wine and gave thanks for it:

Reader 3: Blessed are you, O Lord our God, King of the universe, who has created the fruit of the vine.

Narrator: He gave the cup to his disciples and said,

Reader 3: This cup is the new covenant to be made in my blood. Whenever you drink it, remember me.

Narrator: Therefore, every time we eat this bread and drink this cup, we proclaim the death of the Lord until he returns in glory.

Reader 1: We proclaim that Jesus is the new Passover lamb.

Reader 2: We proclaim that, as God rescued our ancestors through the blood of a lamb, now he rescues us from slavery to sin and death, by the blood of Jesus, the new Passover lamb.

Reader 3: We proclaim a feast in honour of the Lord, at which all, without condition, are welcome at the table of Jesus of Nazareth.

Narrator: Come to his table, share the cup and break the bread. Have done with the past, that you may live, that you may tell your children of all the wonderful things God has done for us.

Narrator
Blessed are you!
Blessed are you!
Blessed are you, O Lord our God!
Blessed are you, O Lord our God!
Blessed are you, O Lord our God, who in Jesus invites us to your table.
Blessed are you, O Lord our God, who in Jesus invites us to your table.

The assembly sings: 'It is a thing most wonderful'

During the singing of the hymn, the table is prepared for the eucharist, and the gifts and people are censed.

The presiding minister continues with the eucharistic prayer

At the end of the eucharistic prayer:
. . . for yours is the power and the glory for ever.

Reader 1: We proclaim a feast in honour of the Lord. Come to his table.
Share the cup and the broken loaf. Come out of your bondage to sin and death and live, so you may be able to tell your children about the wonders the Lord has done for us.

Narrator
Blessed are you.
Blessed are you.
Blessed are you, O Lord our God.
Blessed are you, O Lord our God.
Blessed are you, O Lord, our God. You have saved us and freed us for your kindness' sake.
Blessed are you, O Lord our God. You have saved us and freed us for your kindness' sake.

The assembly sings: 'Broken for me' (Janet Lunt)

The foot-washing

Although some dismiss this ritual as an empty gesture, given that it has no relation to our cultural context, it nevertheless continues to be for most people a moving and powerful symbol. Its potential for spillage or embarrassment is perhaps the very thing that gives the foot-washing its power, for those who perform it in some sense lay themselves bare.

The narrative continues with the passage from John 13 describing how Jesus interrupted the meal in order to model for his followers the way of costly leadership he wants them to imitate in their dealings with others. At the words relating how Jesus 'got up from table, took off his outer robe, and tied a towel around himself', the president does likewise, and those assisting come forward in readiness with the bowl and ewer of (warmed) water.

The precise method of foot-washing will vary, and there are several practical considerations to bear in mind. First, who is involved: the whole assembly, or a token proportion, for example a group of twelve? Second, who ministers this 'sacrament' of Christ's servanthood: the president, or all the clergy, or do the members of the assembly minister to one another?

Theological considerations suggest that it is most fitting (because after all this liturgical gesture is concerned primarily with transforming our understanding of leadership) for the foot-washing to be undertaken by the president, assisted by other clergy as and when necessary, for example if numbers are large or if the president's joints have grown creaky (constantly getting up and down and carrying a bowl of ever-increasing weight can become something of an endurance test as the years take their toll).

It also seems desirable that the whole assembly, not just a token few, is invited to participate. All are called to discipleship, and as Peter discovered (John 13.8–10), the foot-washing is as much about receiving as giving. Furthermore, the choice of a token few is both potentially contentious in pastoral terms, and because ever since that first night, making distinctions within the group carries with it connotations of treachery and betrayal: '"And you are all clean, though not all of you." For he knew who was to betray him; for this reason he said, "Not all of you are clean"' (John 13.10–11).

Such details apart, it remains absolutely essential that, whatever the difficulties or initial reluctance, the foot-washing takes place on this night in any assembly attempting to enter fully and deeply into Holy Week. There is really no excuse for not incorporating the foot-washing into the liturgy of Maundy Thursday night, no matter what the parish may or may not have experienced in previous years.

The biggest obstacle is more often than not uncertainty or embarrassment on the part of the president, especially in circumstances where this ritual is to be introduced for the first time. There is, however, no alternative but to plough ahead undaunted, like John Bunyan's pilgrim. In pioneering the rite where it is not yet known, the trick is to avoid discussing it beforehand as an idea (fatal!) but simply to let it be known, quietly but firmly, that this is what all Christian communities need to practise on this night in obedience to our Lord's command, making clear that this is how things will be from now on.

Particularly when initiating this rite in a local assembly, but also in most other circumstances, it is preferable for the president to go to the people rather than vice versa. This method is not only a more complete modelling of servanthood, but it also exerts gentle pressure towards full participation, requiring members of the assembly to opt out rather than opt in. On the first year, it may well be advisable to plant in the congregation one or two willing souls to be ready to roll, with shoes and socks off, as soon as the rite begins, but in subsequent years that will be found to be entirely unnecessary, such is the power of this moving ceremony for all who take part.

Where numbers are large, it obviously becomes inconsiderate for the president to insist on washing everyone's feet, thereby inevitably condemning the assembly to a prolonged period of waiting. For this reason assistants should be invited to minister also, and when no other clergy are available, senior lay leaders should assist, but by virtue of their office rather than their personal qualities, to avoid subjective selection. As a general guide, a liturgical minister can minister the rite to around 25 people, efficiently but unhurriedly, without undue delay to the whole liturgy.

Music should always be used throughout the foot-washing, to cover any unavoidable noise and to engage in worship those waiting their turn. 'My song is love unknown' is an obvious hymn choice at this moment, and there are many others similar in mood.

The Eucharist

Once the foot-washing is completed and the ministers have returned to their places, the narrative continues with the portion of Scripture taken from Paul's first letter to Corinth, the earliest account we have of the institution of the eucharist. This account having been read to the assembly by the group of readers, a corporal is spread at the president's place at the head of the table and the eucharistic elements are placed on the table, while an appropriate hymn is sung.

The president censes the gifts and then, very slowly and solemnly, the assembly, going round the whole body of the assembly in such a way that each individual is recognized and affirmed as a disciple of Christ.

The eucharistic prayer then follows, and the version that undoubtedly seems most appropriate for this night is the earliest text the Church has, that contained in the *Didache*, dating most probably from the first century. Interestingly, in its form and character this prayer of blessing over bread and wine is heavily Jewish, consolidating our connection with all that has gone before on this night, and the absence of the words of institution from this prayer (although heard a few minutes previously in the reading from First Corinthians) hammers home this point.

At the end of the eucharistic prayer, the readers complete the composite reading with the acclamations. After an appropriate moment of silence, the president invites the assembly to join hands and to recite the Lord's Prayer. The president then breaks the bread and says the fraction sentence. In the setting of this night, the fraction sentence of the American Prayer Book is particularly poignant: 'Christ our Passover is sacrificed for us', to which the people reply 'therefore let us keep the feast'.

Assistants then bring to the table an appropriate number of bowls or small baskets for the bread, and cups for the wine, to allow for the dispersal of the sacrament throughout the assembly. The method of communion will vary from community to community, but it is strongly recommended that on this night, whatever the method chosen, it should differ from the normal practice of the assembly concerned.

Because whatever method chosen will be new or at least different for many of those present, the president will need to issue clear and careful instructions as to how exactly communion is to be shared. One suggestion is as follows.

First, the bread is distributed either directly to each communicant by the eucharistic ministers, or by one communicant to the next, until all members of the assembly are holding in their hands a piece of the consecrated bread. It is essential that the president makes clear that no one should consume the sacrament until invited to do so by the president. Once all have in their hands a piece of the bread, the president announces the words of administration (preferably in this instance simply 'the Body of Christ') and all consume. It is a powerful moment of solidarity among the disciples of our own generation. Silence is maintained throughout.

Once all have received the bread, a sufficient number of cups of consecrated wine are taken by the assistants and placed at regular intervals down the length of the table. Again, the assembly is asked to await instructions from the president before going forward to receive, and the silence is maintained. Once the cups are in place, the president asks of the assembly the same question asked by Jesus of James and John (Matthew 20.22): 'Are you able to drink of the cup that I am about to drink?' To which the assembly responds, using the same reply as the sons of Zebedee on that occasion, 'We are able.' The president then invites the assembly to step forward to the table and to take a cup into their own hands in order to partake of the sacrament. The silence is maintained until all have communicated.

After communion, the assembly sings an appropriate song while the cups are cleared away and the ablutions completed. 'Broken for me, broken for you' or 'This is my body broken for you' are particularly apt at this point.

Where a consecrated host is to be used as the focus of prayer at the altar of repose, this should of course have been consecrated at this eucharist, and after communion placed in a standing pyx or monstrance, covered with a white cloth and placed on a small table to one side. Immediately before the eucharist of Maundy Thursday night, the sacrament in the aumbry or tabernacle should have been consumed by the priest, and the door of the place of reservation left open, revealing the empty chamber.

Once the eucharistic elements have been consumed (save for the host for the altar of repose) and the vessels and candles cleared away, the president says the post-communion prayer. The mood then changes to a darker tone.

The stripping of the altar

The assistants come forward and begin to strip the tables of their white cloths as Psalm 22 is sung. The fact that the tables thereby revealed may look very much less than elegant adds to the pathos of the moment. At the same time assistants remove from the liturgical space all icons, statues, candlesticks and all other liturgical furnishings. The basic rule is, if it is movable, it goes.

The liturgical space should be left looking empty and forlorn, powerfully expressive of the abandonment of Christ by his followers. This is one moment of the year when those of us with minimalist liturgical spaces lose out – there is nothing left to strip! This is especially so when the altar table is a beautiful piece of furniture in its own right, rather than something which only makes a statement if smothered in liturgical petticoats; 'before' and 'after' may look very much the same. It should be regarded as a small price to pay, however, for a space which at all other times of the year succeeds in its purpose of enhancing the liturgy it accommodates.

For Psalm 22 there are of course a wide variety of settings available, but priority should be given to creating a mood of poignant anguish while remaining within the musical scope of the assembly.

The Gethsemane watch

After the stripping of the altar tables, a corporal is spread on the table in front of the president, who places on it the monstrance or standing pyx containing the host. The president dons a humeral veil or, if none is available, a white cloth around the shoulders, and censes the Blessed Sacrament. The president then takes up the monstrance or standing pyx and holds it high before him/her.

A procession forms, led by the thurifer, with the acolytes walking directly in front of the president carrying the Blessed Sacrament or, if space permits, on either side, followed by the whole assembly. The ancient plainsong hymn 'Sing my tongue, the mystery telling' is sung by the assembly as it wends its way to the altar of repose.

The altar of repose will be a table set up in a separate place at some distance from the place where the sacred meal has just been celebrated, the movement to which will recapture for the assembly some sense of the journey by the disciples from the upper room to the place called Gethsemane. Local circumstances will determine where this place apart is best located, and it is good to be creative. Sometimes a side chapel in a large church building will suffice, or perhaps the far east end of the building (as at Philadelphia Cathedral) precisely because it is a portion of the church building rarely used at any other time of the year.

Going further, it may well make more of a statement if our own Gethsemane is less convenient and more exposed. It might be located in a narthex, or porch, or gallery, or a room in a church hall. Weather permitting, it might even be outside in a court-yard or garden.

It is helpful to our imaginations, and pastorally helpful as a means of involving members of the assembly, if the room or space selected for this purpose is to some degree transformed into a garden for this night. It remains, however, a question of degree. The end result should recall or suggest a garden but not proclaim one. This is not Chelsea Flower Show but a minimalist sketch of a vacant lot in a Middle East city in winter. Branches, not blossoms, are the order of the day; Easter, though it is coming, has not yet arrived.

A simple table forms the centrepiece of the 'garden', on which a corporal is spread, with a sufficient number of candles placed on either side, producing the effect of simple dignity rather than excessive formality. The candles should provide just suffi-cient light in the room or space concerned, supplemented by artificial light only in so far as necessary for safe coming and going. The 'garden' should remain predomi-nantly open, with just sufficient furniture to facilitate different options for private prayer without cluttering the place; a few stools or upright chairs, some cushions on the floor, a bench or two at the perimeter.

At the end of the procession from the place of celebration, the Blessed Sacrament is placed here to serve as the focus of the prayer of the assembly through the watch of prayer until midnight. In faith communities where the Blessed Sacrament plays no part in their spirituality, an alternative focus of prayer will need to be devised. On the eve of the day of crucifixion a cross should be avoided, as this will come into its own the next day, and indeed any image or representation of Christ seems somehow inadequate and too limiting in this moment (a criticism that many of course may level against the Sacrament also). Perhaps a circle of small candles on the floor is all that is needed to give wings to our prayer.

Maundy Thursday: the Gethsemane watch at the altar of repose

Whatever vehicle is chosen to focus our prayer, the Gethsemane watch presents any pastor with a superb opportunity to teach faithfulness in prayer and discipleship. 'Could you not keep awake one hour?' were the words of Jesus in reproach to his hapless followers in the first Gethsemane. Ever since, his disciples of subsequent generations have attempted to do better, and in some small way to make up what was lacking in the first batch.

It is helpful to teach the importance of this time well before the event, and to display on previous Sundays a rota of prayer times until midnight to ensure a good number of people present throughout the period. A moment should also be taken during the liturgy of Maundy Thursday night to emphasize yet again the importance of this time, and the significance of this liturgy which ends, not in coffee and conversation, but in silent prayer and dispersion into the night. After the eucharistic liturgy, the assembly remains in silence at the altar of repose, or departs in silence to return to pray later. There is no talking, and the lights of the church interior should be dimmed to a level equivalent to emergency lighting, sufficient only for safe exit.

Where the Blessed Sacrament is used, the president, having placed the monstrance or pyx on the altar of repose, leads the assembly in kneeling before the Sacrament in silent adoration, and then censes it. The president and other sacred ministers then withdraw in silence.

The Gethsemane watch of prayer continues until midnight, at which time the president or other minister kneels before the altar of repose and reads the New Testament narrative of the end of Jesus' own agonized vigil of prayer (such as, Mark 14.32–42), ending with the words, 'Get up, let us be going. See, my betrayer is at hand.' The president then removes the Blessed Sacrament from the altar of repose, carries it to the sacristy, where it is reverently consumed. The candles are extinguished and the assembly disperses in silence.

See-at-a-glance Liturgy of the Last Supper

Entrance
Greeting and explanation
Prayer of the day
The reading of the Scriptures
(a) the account of the Exodus: the assembly tastes the Passover food
(b) the account of the foot-washing: the president washes the feet of members of the assembly
(c) the account of the institution of the eucharist: the assembly breaks bread and shares a cup of wine

The stripping of the altar
The procession of the Blessed Sacrament to the altar of repose
The Gethsemane watch of prayer
Dispersal in silence

Music for the Eucharist of the Last Supper

See Appendix 3 for full publication details.

Entrance song

'Lift high the cross', in *The Hymnal 1982*.

Gloria

'Gloria', William Matthias, in *The Hymnal 1982*.

Lighting of the lamps

'Kindle a flame', Iona Community, in *Ritual Song*.

Refrain for Passover narrative

'Bless the Lord, my soul' (3 times), Taizé, in *Complete Anglican Hymns Old & New*.

Song at conclusion of Passover meal

'Will you let me be your servant?' ('The servant song'), Richard Gillard, in *Gather* and *Celebration Hymnal for Everyone*.

Song at the foot-washing

'My song is love unknown', John Ireland, in *The Hymnal 1982*.

Choral reflection

'God so loved the world', J. Stainer.

Song at conclusion of foot-washing

'It is a thing most wonderful' (tune: 'Herongate'), in *The New English Hymnal*.

Song at conclusion of eucharistic prayer

'Broken for me, broken for you', Janet Lunt, in *Complete Anglican Hymns Old and New*.

Song at the breaking of the bread

'There is something holy here', Christopher Walker, OCP Publications (sheet music).

Communion song

'This is my body, broken for you', Jimmy Owens, in *The Complete Celebration Hymnal*.

Stripping of the altar

Psalm 22, Christopher Tambling, in *Sunday Psalms*.
'My god, my God', Liam Lawton, GIA Publications (sheet music).

Procession to the altar of repose

'Sing, my tongue, the glorious battle' (*Pange lingua*), in *The New English Hymnal*.

At the Gethsemane garden

'Silent, surrendered', Margaret Rizza, in *Be Still and Know*.
'Tantum Ergo', (tune: Grafton), in *The New English Hymnal*.

GOOD FRIDAY
Historical background

This is the most solemn day of the year, though its character as we know it today represents a departure from primitive Christian custom. Originally the *Pasch*, the Christian version of the Passover, was a single unitive commemoration of both the death and the resurrection of Christ. Only later was the commemoration of the cross detached and given a day of its own, probably because by the fourth century the custom of weekly fasting on Fridays had become general, and the Friday fast before the *Pasch* had naturally to outdo them all.

Characteristics

Today Good Friday is with Ash Wednesday one of the two chief days when the Church gets really serious about prayer and fasting, but yet one which presents more of a challenge to the Church in terms of meaningful observance, largely because it is in Western culture treated as an ordinary working day.

The question of how best to mark this most solemn of days in the Church's Year continues to vary depending on local tradition and circumstances. For those churches which pride themselves on being liturgical, the only satisfactory solution is the solemn celebration of the Liturgy of Good Friday, which more and more gains acceptance as the norm. Even here, however, there remain some important decisions about what should be included or omitted.

Until recently the Three Hours Devotion between 12 p.m. and 3 p.m., the traditional hours of crucifixion, remained a popular option. This was a non-liturgical service of meditations on a scriptural theme (for example the sayings of Christ from the cross), interspersed with hymns and periods of silence. The devotion was divided up into sections, and people came and went for whatever periods of time they had available. It was very much an individualistic affair rather than a corporate act, and has gradually faded in popularity.

One reason for this has been the greatly increased use of the traditional Liturgy of Good Friday Liturgy simplified and re-presented for congregations in the official liturgical material published by the mainstream churches in Britain and the USA. Whereas thirty years ago the observance of the Liturgy of Good Friday was perforce an exercise in liturgical disloyalty, today this Liturgy has been given wide circulation, first in *Lent, Holy Week and Easter* (1984) and more recently in *Common Worship: Times and Seasons* (2006). The Episcopal Church was ahead of the curve, including the full Good Friday ceremonies in its new *Book of Common Prayer* (1979).

Cultural context

The second reason for a decline in the observance of the Three Hours, or other equivalent services attempting to follow the timetable of the first Good Friday, has been the increasing secularization of the day. Although Good Friday remains in Britain technically a Bank Holiday, it is less and less observed. This means that the Church needs must choose between a ritual observance at the 'proper' time (traditionally held to be 3 p.m.), involving predominantly the retired and the very young, or one at a time unrelated to the supposed hour of crucifixion but potentially involving the whole community of faith.

The latter option is gradually but irreversibly gaining ground, with the main observance of Good Friday tending to be in the evening, after work, with a lesser observance at the traditional daytime hours. This may involve maintaining a vigil of prayer from 12 p.m. until 3 p.m., which marks also the customary end of the Good Friday fast. Such a vigil may or may not include short periods of guided prayer on the hour or half-hour.

Setting

The first requirement for the worship team is of course to clear away early the last vestiges of the liturgies of Maundy Thursday. Where the stripping of the altars has been rigorously carried out the previous evening, this will involve nothing much more than removing all signs of the Gethsemane garden.

Good Friday: the liturgical space expresses emptiness and desolation

The liturgy demands nothing more, in liturgical space terms, than wide open space, sufficient chairs for the people present, and a suitable place for veneration. Depending on whether or not communion will be given, an altar table may or may not be necessary.

The seating configuration should require of the assembly a sense of engagement in the terrible events recalled in the liturgy; no one should be allowed to imagine they are merely spectators of some ghastly spectacle occurring long ago. One way of achieving this is for the basic long rectangle of the 'upper room' configuration of Maundy Thursday night to be retained, perhaps pushing back the chairs to create a wider central aisle, empty of furniture save for the ambo at the west end.

Choreography

It is good to offer the public recitation of Morning Prayer on this day, albeit in a severely truncated form. It should begin directly with Psalm 22, without introductory versicles and responses, or doxologies. The invitatory *Venite*, Psalm 95, seems particularly inappropriate on Good Friday, and should also be omitted.

The chief components of the Liturgy of Good Friday are the reading or singing of

John's account of the Passion of Christ, the Solemn Prayers, and the Veneration of the Cross. To these solemn acts may be added the prostration of the sacred ministers at the beginning of the liturgy, and the communion from the Reserved Sacrament.

The prostration

The Liturgy begins dramatically. The assembly stands, and the sacred ministers, in albs and red vestments, enter in silence, proceed slowly up the wide central aisle, and at a prearranged point fall to the ground to lie prostrate before God – perhaps we may say the God of absence on this aweful day. The drama lies in the total absence of the means by which we normally create a sense of the dramatic. Silence replaces tumultuous celebratory sound, abject prostration replaces movement and ceremony. Because these actions are reserved for this day alone, they never fail to exert an immense impact on the assembly.

The introduction

The president and other ministers then move to their chairs, and it is most effective if these are placed, not in a special place of honour, but simply as part of the rectangle formed by the rest of the chairs, alongside the other members of the assembly.

The president reads the prayer of the day (singing on this day should be restricted to the Passion) and the assembly sits for the first reading. After a suitable period of silence, the psalm is sung, and the second reading follows. After a further period of silence those involved in the singing of the Passion make their way to the ambo.

The Passion

The Passion should be sensibly shortened to cut out the whole section dealing with the arrest and the denial by Peter (John 18.1–27) and to concentrate on the trial before Pilate and the crucifixion (John 18.28—19.42). This is common sense, especially where there is some pressure of time, as when the noon hour is used and participants may be on a lunch break. Furthermore, the singing of the Passion is not an endurance test, but a means of reawakening us to the terrible events of that day, and holding us alert and transfixed.

It is good if there are sufficient voices to allow one for each part, with three as an absolute minimum. Traditionally, a priest sings the Christus part, but this should no longer be considered de rigueur as we gradually emerge from our clericalist ways. The traditional chant remains hauntingly evocative, and will be hard to beat, although the translation can at certain points seem somewhat banal.

The assembly should be invited to sit during the Passion, so as to better concentrate on the content and message of what is being sung, but should rise and stand in silence with heads bowed at the moment of Christ's death. This movement will be indicated by a gesture from the chief cantor and by the liturgical ministers taking a lead.

At the end of the Passion the cantors return to their places in the assembly, and the assembly is seated, silence being maintained throughout. The Passion ends without versicle and response, as they would appear trite. There is no possible response other than stunned silence.

For the same reason a homily is usually superfluous. For much of the Church's history, the need to 'preach the cross' would have been regarded as an essential means of convicting a congregation of its sin and its need for repentance. Today it is safe to say that for many Christians the jury is out on the concept of Jesus as the new Isaac, the victim to be sacrificed by his own father. The contemporary believer is more likely to see the readiness of Abraham to sacrifice his son as some gruesome misguided attempt to appease a vengeful God, rather than as a model for the self-offering of Jesus the Christ. Silence speaks more powerfully, and can touch more hearts, than any number of theories of substitutionary atonement.

Following an appropriate period of silence after the Passion, therefore, the liturgy moves us on to a fitting response. In the past this took the form of intercessory prayer in the shape of the solemn collects, the traditional prayers for various sorts and conditions of humankind for whom on this day we make special intercession before the cross. These are of ancient origin, their form following the pattern of the intercessions from the early Roman eucharistic rite.

Common Worship: Times and Seasons (2006), however, suggests a reversion to the earlier tradition of the Ambrosian rite of Milan, in which the Passion is followed, far more appropriately, by action rather than words. The veneration (or proclamation) of the cross thus comes first, and then the solemn collects (prayers of intercession).

Proclamation of the cross

The proclamation of the cross (as *Common Worship: Times and Seasons* (2006) helpfully renames it), used once upon a time to be one of those 'naughty' liturgical practices by which a parish of the Catholic tradition was recognized as 'full faith'. As late as 1905 Archbishop Randall Davidson, in giving evidence before the Royal Commission on Church Discipline, cited the veneration of the cross as one of those 'unauthorized and inadmissible' and 'most undesirable' services which succeeded in getting the whole Church worked up into a rare state of excitement, and which caused the Protestant agitator Mr Kensit to foam at the mouth (Bell, 1952, p. 467).

Such Establishment censure inevitably ensured that 'veneration' became something of a badge of honour among parishes of the Catholic tradition. Even in the 1960s it was still considered rather daring and 'extreme', and in my training parish this Good Friday devotion was promoted avidly, with many an appeal to parallels in daily life, for example the very natural habit of kissing the photograph of an absent loved one.

The proclamation (in some places once called the 'Creeping to the Cross' – now there's a public relations nightmare!) is however no recent invention of the ritualistic movement, and enjoys a good liturgical pedigree. It is described in the *Pilgrimage of Egeria* (around 382 CE) as one of the rites of Holy Week in Jerusalem at that time. At first it was associated with the veneration of the true relics of the 'true cross', but gradually spread throughout the Christian world, at first to places other than Jerusalem that claimed to possess a beam of the true cross, then to those who had merely a mote, and then everywhere.

Veneration is one of those practices or areas of the Church's life (a bit like praying for the departed) for which the pure Protestant cause is doomed from the start. It is better to admit defeat and run with it. For the Christian believer who takes to heart the awful story of the torture and execution of the beloved Master, something more is needed on this day than a cerebral appreciation of the finer points of salvation theology. In human terms we need to go the graveside or hold close a memento or at least kiss a photograph of the departed loved one. This is what veneration allows us to do in a liturgical setting, and it never fails to move and inspire, as much in the observance of one's fellow pilgrims as in the act itself.

The proclamation begins with the deacon or other liturgical minister withdrawing to the narthex or other separate, or at least distinct, space to take up a suitable crucifix and to enter the liturgical space flanked by torch-bearers. The crucifix (preferable in this case to a plain cross) should be large enough to stand alone in the space, while being light enough to be carried.

Usually we think of a cross small enough to be carried by one person, but at the Norbertine monastery of Daylesford Abbey, Pennsylvania, a full-size cross is carried in horizontally on the shoulders of eight young people walking in silence – a sight which moves many to tears.

Care should be taken to find a crucifix which is neither lurid in appearance or cheaply made, and if there is not one such on display at other times in the parish, then one should be acquired specifically for this purpose and kept at other times in the sacristy.

The crucifix is held aloft and proclaimed at three stations between the entrance and the place of veneration, the deacon singing at each station, 'Behold the wood of the cross on which hung the saviour of the world', to which the people reply, 'Come let us worship!'

It remains the custom in many places to veil the cross (in white on this occasion) and to remove the veil by stages, revealing a little more of the crucifix at each station. For many today, however, this smacks a little too much of the dance of the seven veils, somehow trivializing the moment, and it is preferable for the cross to be unveiled throughout in stark reminder of what we are witnessing.

When the deacon arrives at the place of veneration, the crucifix is placed in a stand in a position which enables the faithful to come and kneel in adoration and to kiss the feet of the Christ figure, or at least kneel in rapt devotion before it. For this, the essential requirement is a stand that is sturdy and which fits the crucifix, so that it doesn't wobble or even fall over, causing consternation and embarrassment. The practice of having acolytes at either side to keep things on an even keel is intrusive, and a way should be found to allow the crucifix to stand without supports, providing a private moment for the worshipper.

The deacon, having placed the cross in the stand, then steps back to allow the president to go first and to set the example, followed by the other liturgical ministers. The assembly is then invited to follow. No intrusive stage direction is required here, but simply a few well-trained members of the assembly showing the way.

During the proclamation, suitable hymns and songs should be sung, and this is a good time to be enfolded by comforting favourites such as 'When I survey the wondrous cross', or 'There is a green hill far away', or for a soloist to sing a piece such as 'Were you there when they crucified my Lord?' *Common Worship: Times and Seasons* (2006) also sets out the more traditional anthems, made up predominantly of scriptural material. A pastoral decision will need to be made here between words of haunting beauty (probably sung to unfamiliar music), and tunes of emotive power (probably set to over-familiar words).

Prayers of intercession

When all the members of the assembly wishing to come forward have done so, a further period of silence ensues, before the president at the chair introduces the prayers of intercession.

The prayers work methodically through the major areas of the Church's concern, from its own unity and faithfulness, to the nations of the earth, the suffering, and the unbelieving. These intercessions have now come of age, having been purged of previous attempts, lingering from a bygone age, to take the opportunity on this day to take a swipe at all those we wish to blame or consign to hellfire, among which Jews, Turks and Infidels were always top of the pops as handy targets.

The prayers of intercession consist of biddings for each section followed, after a hefty period of silence, by a related set prayer. They are prefaced by an introductory invitation said by a deacon or other assisting minister. The biddings are usually said by that same minister, and the collects themselves by the president. In days gone by there was much bobbing up and down, the assembly standing for the biddings and kneeling for the prayers, but except for the most exotic of liturgical locations, that is now gone. It is more seemly and prayerful if the assembly stands reverently throughout, concentrating its energies on attentive listening rather than the acrobatic flexing of calf-muscles.

The prayers of intercession should be separated from the closing prayers to avoid too wordy a conclusion, and a contemporary song such as Roger Jones's 'I met you at the cross' serves very well. After this the president leads the assembly in the Lord's Prayer and then one of the two prayers of the conclusion. After this the liturgical ministers depart, not in procession, but in a higgledy-piggledy manner appropriate to the disarray and desolation of the day.

Holy Communion

Alternatively, the liturgy may conclude with the distribution of the Holy Communion (in one kind only) from the Reserved Sacrament, in an ancient rite, attested to from the eighth century, known as the Mass of the Presanctified. Before the current round of liturgical renewal this rite was another litmus test of any parish claiming to provide full Catholic privileges; a *sine qua non* of liturgical orthodoxy. Today we are in a better place to come to an unpressured decision about what is most appropriate.

While in the Western Church the reception of Holy Communion on a daily basis has for centuries been the mark of the truly devout, no one would suppose that a celebration of the eucharist on Good Friday could even be considered, for such an act would seem arrogant and distasteful.

It seems, however, that from the eighth century at least, humankind was considered so frail and indigent that special arrangements had to be made to ensure that not for one single day should the faithful be deprived of the Sacrament. Although it is true that until the reform of the Roman Holy Week Rites in 1955, communion on this occasion was restricted to the celebrant alone, the reforms of that year reinstated the general communion which was the practice of the early Middle Ages. The faithful must not go without!

Although this custom has a good pedigree in both the Eastern and Western

Church, to modern sensibilities it can appear a little self-indulgent. Is there not a single day in the year when restraint trumps our neediness? R. F. Buxton (in Davies (ed.), 1986, p. 252) points out that this custom detracts both from the day's 'powerful bareness and simplicity, with its note of desolation . . . and from the Easter liturgy and communion to which celebration of the passion and death looks forward'.

Is there not something just a little pathetic in this demand, however ancient the provision may be? If we are going to take it seriously, let Good Friday be a day of fasting and real spiritual hunger.

Where, however, we wish to continue this custom, the deacon or other liturgical minister goes at this point to the place of Reservation and, flanked by acolytes, carries in procession the ciborium containing the hosts consecrated on a previous occasion. The ciborium is placed on a corporal spread on the altar table, and the president leads the assembly in the Lord's Prayer. The American *Book of Common Prayer* (1979) stipulates that a general confession should preface the Lord's Prayer, but this seems liturgically superfluous in view of all that has gone before.

Holy Communion is then administered in the usual way, the ciborium is cleansed, and the closing prayer said before the ministers depart.

See-at-a-glance Liturgy of Good Friday

Chair

Entrance – in silence
Prostration

Ambo

Prayer of the day
Reading from the Hebrew Scriptures
Psalm
Reading from the Christian Scriptures

The Passion

The proclamation of the cross

The prayers of intercession

[Holy Communion]

The Lord's Prayer

Conclusion

Music for Good Friday

See Appendix 3 for full publishing details.

Psalm

Psalm 22, Christopher Tambling, in *Sunday Psalms*.

At the proclamation of the cross

'O sacred head' (Passion chorale), in *The Hymnal 1982* and *The New English Hymnal*.
'When I survey the wondrous cross' (tune: 'Rockingham'), in *The Hymnal 1982*.

After the prayers of intercession

'I met you at the cross', Roger Jones, in *The Complete Celebration Hymnal*.

HOLY SATURDAY
Characteristics

Holy Saturday (Easter Eve) is a day with a character of its own which deserves to be savoured but rarely is. It is a day when the pain is over and the waiting and wondering begins. Hope peeps its head over the parapet, only to be dragged back down again by doubt and fear.

We are provided with orders of Morning and Evening Prayer appropriate for the day, and we should not ignore them. For the committed, Holy Saturday is a day of intense preparation, with a fire to be laid, a liturgical space to be transformed, music to be practised, and catechumens to be rehearsed.

Choreography

All this should begin quietly and prayerfully with Morning Prayer, and every effort should be made to make the praying of the Divine Office the first thing the community does together before the coffee urn goes on and the frantic dashing about begins.

The office is short and restrained on this day, but therefore all the more powerful.

Likewise Evening Prayer might be a very good way to bring the work of preparation to an end, before the troops go home to put their feet up for an hour or, more likely, rush off to do last-minute shopping. Care should be taken to keep a safe liturgical distance between Evening Prayer and any liturgies later that same evening forming the first part of the Easter Vigil. The distinct character of Evening Prayer on Easter Eve needs to be preserved, being in no way an anticipation of the first celebration of Easter itself.

Notes

1 There are many excellent books available setting out the Haggadah, and the primary source here is the work of Joy Levitt and Michael Strassfeld, entitled *A Night of Questions* (Elkins Park, PA, Reconstructionist Press, 2000).

2 Mordecai Kaplan, quoted in Levitt and Strassfeld, *A Night of Questions*, p. 9.

3 Levitt and Strassfeld, *A Night of Questions*, p. 11.

4 Levitt and Strassfeld, *A Night of Questions*, p. 11.

7 EASTER DAY

Easter Vigil: the proclamation of the Exsultet

Historical background

The joyful observance of Easter Day, proclaiming that Christ is raised, is the centre-piece of the whole cycle of the Church's Year. The *Pasch*, the Christian Passover, was originally a unified commemoration of both cross and resurrection, but by the end of the fourth century the commemoration of the death of Christ had been hived off into a day in its own right (Good Friday), leaving the *Pasch* associated with the theme of resurrection alone.

The way in which we celebrate Easter is of the utmost importance both in terms of the formation of the faithful and the evangelization of those yet to be incorporated into the Church's life. For the pastor and those planning the Easter ceremonies, this brings to the fore crucial policy decisions not devoid of pastoral repercussions.

When viewed in relationship to all that has gone before, *Common Worship: Times and Seasons* (2006) transports us to a new liturgical planet, where for the first time since the Reformation it is assumed that the local church will wish to 'embrace and ever hold fast' the fullest and deepest celebration of the Easter mysteries, rather than cobble them together from materials smuggled in from other communions. Like citizens welcoming the Restoration, we can at last go public with our true allegiance after a long period of oppressive seriousness and deprivation. Let the street parties begin.

Characteristics

The two strands intertwined throughout the traditional Easter celebration are those of recalling past events and experiencing present reality. These involve storytelling and encounter, quiet reflection and joyous celebration, and neither should push the other to the edge of our Easter experience. It is no good simply extolling glorious deeds and events of a bygone age, nor will it do to allow our celebration to be ephemeral or shallow, ungrounded in history. Both strands need to be woven into the assembly's taking hold of the Easter event, passing from darkness into light, from death into life.

The liturgical observance of the feast of the resurrection of Christ has several components, and nomenclature for this liturgical extravaganza can get complicated. Although the Vigil is strictly speaking but one element of the whole Easter Liturgy, the name usually given to the whole bang shoot is nevertheless The Easter Vigil. In the American *Book of Common Prayer* (1979) indeed, the whole celebration is called The Great Vigil of Easter. This has resonance and style but perpetuates a degree of confusion in that the Vigil proper forms but one element out of four.

Common Worship: Times and Seasons (2006), on the other hand, refers to the whole resurrection liturgy as the Easter Liturgy, and this is the name that will be given here to the whole liturgical celebration which of course includes the Vigil itself.

With commendable clarity *Common Worship: Times and Seasons* (2006) sets out (p. 326) the four main components of the Easter Liturgy, set out below in their customary order. The character and purpose of each of these constituent parts, and the relationship and balance between them, needs to be constantly borne in mind as we plan our Easter celebration.

The Vigil

A vigil is a watchful keeping awake during a time usually given to sleep, and the Church's Vigil through the night leading into the commemoration of Christ's resurrection is of ancient provenance. In this Christian Vigil of Easter, the Church would keep watch while praying and mulling over the stories from the Scriptures of God's saving acts of mercy and might towards God's chosen and beloved people.

Because the discovery of Christ's resurrection was stumbled onto by his women followers 'while it was still dark', the Vigil traditionally continued until dawn, culminating in the acclamation of the Risen Lord as day broke. It is therefore a true vigil of the night, and if we are to have any authentic experience of the Vigil we should eschew any sissy stuff such as half-vigils of the twilight hours. We either go for it or we don't.

Versions of the Easter Vigil that end before the night is over are also problematic. They are elaborate exercises in anti-climax, requiring participants to return home in the middle of the night, celebrating a theoretical and cerebral resurrection while the wee small hours are yet to come, with all their anxiety, doubt and fear, and the new light and warmth of dawn remains a distant uncertainty.

The Service of Light

Light in all its forms, no less than the dawn, became from the earliest moments of the Church a potent symbol of Christ's new life. The Service of Light proclaims the resurrection in deed rather than word, using, in the context of the Vigil's darkness, a lighted candle as the simplest and most powerful of all visual aids. The Easter (or Paschal) Candle is lit from the new fire and brought into the darkened church building to symbolize Christ, the light of the world.

By means of individual candles held by each member of the assembly, the light is gradually passed from this single flame into the darkest corners of the building, just as Christ penetrates with the radiance of his presence the darkest corners of the earth. The Exsultet, the ancient song in praise of the Easter Candle, brings the Service of Light to a triumphal end.

The Liturgy of Initiation

From earliest times, the Church used the Easter Vigil and the period leading up to it as the doorway into the new life experienced by the followers of Jesus Christ. The symbolic movement from death to life was embodied not only in the rite of baptism itself, with its experience of drowning in, and rising from, the water, but in the whole structure of an Easter celebration emerging from a long period of fasting, prayer and preparation. It was the perfect vehicle for an initiation process in which actions spoke just as loudly as words; death and resurrection were lived into, not just theorized about. This dramatic experience of entering into the Christian way made an impact which was likely to be profound and lasting.

The Easter Vigil is therefore the supremely appropriate time in the Church's annual cycle for incorporating new members by baptism and/or confirmation. Should no candidates be forthcoming, the public Re-affirmation of Baptismal Vows by the whole assembly serves to keep the theme of initiation and discipleship as a primary element in the Easter Vigil experience.

The Eucharist

The disciples who encountered the Risen Lord on the road to Emmaus excitedly told to their companions what had happened by explaining that 'he had been made known to them in the breaking of the bread' (Luke 24.35). The Gospel account of this incident shows that, despite a lengthy discourse and exposition of the Scriptures by Jesus on a walk which must have taken some hours, he remained unrecognized. Only when, in the context of their home, he took and blessed and broke bread and shared it with them did the penny drop: this stranger was the Lord.

In many ways the Easter Vigil echoes this experience for us today. Here the community of disciples, the Church, hears over an extended period a rehearsal of the salient points in the story of God's love for us, complete with an interpretation of its meaning, and yet we can remain untouched, unconvinced or unmoved. Only when we come, at the culmination of the whole Easter Liturgy, to gather round the altar table as the household of faith to take, bless, break and share bread, and to bless and share a cup of wine, do the scales fall from our eyes. The pieces all fit together at last, and we recognize the Risen Lord in our midst, and ourselves, mirrored in his face, as the beloved children of God irradiated with his presence and power.

Just as the Vigil is very much a night thing, the eucharist of Easter is a morning thing. We should avoid its celebration during the previous night, let alone the evening before, for this robs us of its powerful connection with the joy of the new dawn, in which Christ is our sun and source of life. Celebrating any liturgy at a time which makes nonsense of the language of the rite and which goes against the grain of its natural setting is but to drive another nail in the coffin of worship related to life.

Timetable options

Looking then at these four constituent parts of the Easter Liturgy, we can discern how over the centuries the Church has developed in different settings different ways of arranging these parts into a meaningful whole. How might we present them in a way which does justice to each element and produces a composite liturgy of grace and power? Assuming we are attempting to incorporate all four parts, the alternatives might be:

- to celebrate the Easter Liturgy as one complete service of four parts during the night, reaching its climax as day breaks.
- to celebrate the Vigil and the Service of Light on Saturday evening, and then after a gap, gather on Easter morning to celebrate the Liturgies of Initiation and of the Eucharist.
- to celebrate the Vigil, perhaps shortened, on Saturday evening or just before dawn on Sunday, and then the other three parts of the Easter Liturgy – the Service of Light, and the Liturgies of Initiation and the Eucharist – later on Easter Day.

In situations where we separate out one or two parts of the Easter Liturgy to stand alone, the challenge is always how to retain a sense of unity between the separated elements as constituent parts of a composite whole.

For parishes where the Easter Day mid-morning service (not necessarily eucharistic) is the best attended event of the year, there is a different challenge which is twofold: how to give participants at least a taste of the liturgical drama being played out across the wider Church, and how to provide an up-beat all-age non-eucharistic worship service while making provision also for the necessary eucharistic celebration which is more than an afterthought or a huddle in a corner for those so inclined.

Common Worship: Times and Seasons (2006) nobly makes provision for a non-eucharistic Service of the Word, and although this incorporates some liturgical elements from parts of the Easter Liturgy, it is something of a slippery slope into wordy religion. This may be entirely laudable for pastoral and evangelistic reasons, but deprives participants of an experience of how Easter has been celebrated for two thousand years.

The trick is to re-present the ancient rites in such a way that, albeit in shortened or simplified form, they engage the interest of newcomers and excite their imagination.

The widespread hunger of people 'out there' for spirituality as opposed to religion is much spoken of, and has indeed taken on legendary proportions. The Easter liturgies give the Church countless opportunities for being 'like the master of a household who brings out of his treasure what is new and what is old' (Matthew 13.52). We have so many good things at our disposal that we are spoilt for choice.

The first issue to resolve is pastoral rather than liturgical, and concerns the place of the Easter Liturgy in the overall plan for celebrating the resurrection event in our local community of faith. Is the Easter Liturgy, Vigil and all, *the* celebration of the presence of the Risen Lord for all members of our local assembly, or is it one option alongside others?

There can be no doubt that the answer should always be the former. The Easter mystery defines our faith and forms our apostleship, and the ancient and dramatic rites of the Easter Liturgy should engage and energize every Christian. It can never be an optional extra or even a preferred alternative for a faith community serious about its liturgical life.

Concerns about participation by particular age or interest groups, young or old or disabled, are challenges to be overcome, not reasons for allowing people to opt out of this central act of the Church's Year. This is no time for fringe services for those we consider are entitled to special treatment or to dumbing down. This is it; the moment has come.

The second question, granted that the Easter Liturgy is to be the central and sole liturgical rite of the whole community, concerns its timing. When exactly should it take place?

The first thought may be to celebrate the Easter Liturgy at the customary time of the main service every Sunday, but although this is the 'default time' most likely to net the maximum number of participants, there are other issues at stake. If the building-up of a mature assembly of believers in touch with their past as well as the present moment, is the aim, then to allow the Easter Liturgy to coincide with the regular Sunday slot represents a short-term gain at the expense of a long-term advance.

The Easter Liturgy is not an event designed to cause us least inconvenience, but one which should turn our life around. It is an event which should demand of us a rethink of a normal Sunday, requiring of us no little upheaval: a note of reminder to ourselves entered in our diary weeks or even months before the event, special arrangements made, friends to be encouraged, and fellow parishioners to be woken on the day with a phone call or collected by car. It is an out-of-the-ordinary event, not typical or regular in any way.

Our second thought may be to fall in with the customary timing favoured by parishes of a Catholic tradition: that is, the full Easter Liturgy celebrated at midnight, or earlier that evening, on Holy Saturday. This will never do. First, the rite at this hour sends you home in the dark, and (to use a favourite American word) discombobulates you entirely. The effect is not dissimilar from that of going to a cinema on a gorgeous sunny afternoon; one emerges at quite the wrong time of day, blinking into bright sunlight. Emerging from the Easter Vigil at one in the morning is a reverse image of the same experience; there is something a little louche and disreputable about it. You are left with an anti-climactic sense that, after all that fuss, Easter is yet to come.

The Easter Liturgy beginning on Saturday evening leaves you also with the problem of Easter Day morning; it leaves a very large hole in the Easter programme. Are we really to stand by and do nothing on Sunday morning? That would be inconceivable. Therefore a Saturday evening slot inevitably consigns the full Easter rites to second best place, the limited preserve of the cognoscenti.

Liturgical options

For the above reasons it may be that we come back, albeit with no little apprehension, to the solution of the early Church: the Easter Liturgy, as a night-into-day experience of the dawn. The women companions of Jesus discovered the empty tomb 'early on the first day of the week while it was still dark' (John 20.1), and we do likewise.

Surely, goes up the cry, this is pastorally unworkable, a no-hoper of a liturgical project? More common is the complaint that 'that's a nice idea, but it would never fly in our parish'. Such assertions are not based on fact, only on defeatism. A dawn Easter Liturgy, at say 5.00 a.m., is in fact a particularly effective way of galvanizing a parish community into a real sense of adventure in its rediscovery of what Easter is all about and, once experienced, it's quite addictive; there's no going back.

A dawn Easter Liturgy has been found to fly in communities as disparate as a sub-urban parish in the South East, an industrial parish in Tyneside, an inner-city parish in West Yorkshire (now there's a challenge!) and in a cathedral on America's Eastern Seaboard. In all cases it needed careful preparation and teaching, and plenty of advance notice, though not of a possibility they may like to discuss, but of a done deal.

The basis for a dawn Easter Liturgy is that this is the most natural thing in the world, for whether it's a child waiting for Father Christmas, or an adult setting off on their first trip to far distant places, a common denominator of excitement and expectation is a restless night and an early start. If it's something we are excited about then we can't wait to be up and ready and to get going. If we are really determined to do so, we can make the dawn Easter Liturgy an all-age experience of worship which will leave its mark upon us for years to come.

Furthermore, this is what the first Christians found to *work* as a means of entering into the Easter mystery. For us today to have a sense of solidarity in our praxis with the Church of the first centuries is an important tool in re-equipping ourselves for life in a post-Christian (as theirs was a pre-Christian) age. We occupy an increasing amount of common ground.

One possible alternative to the dawn event is to split the Easter Liturgy into two, celebrating the new fire, the lighting of the candle, and the Liturgy of the Word after dark on Holy Saturday evening, and then dispersing to gather again early on Easter morning – say 7.00 a.m. or any time other than the normal time for Sunday gathering – to celebrate with the eucharist our entering into the New Covenant. In this instance the Easter morning rite might begin with a reading of the Liturgy of the Word, as a token recapitulation of all that has gone before, using that from the prophet Zephaniah, concerning the gathering of God's people. Then the Liturgy moves directly into the Easter Acclamation, the singing of the Gloria and the first reading from the New Testament.

This arrangement has certain advantages, namely the potential to involve greater numbers and to savour the Liturgy of the Word as a rite in itself, not something to be endured until we get to party time. In this setting the Liturgy of the Word becomes what it was always meant to be: the community's recalling of its sacred story and of God's saving acts. It is a time for storytelling, not just from sacred books millennia old, but from day-to-day life in our own generation. This is what those from the Evangelical tradition would call witnessing, and if ever there was a liturgical setting in which it should be encouraged and given place, this is it.

On balance, however, it seems a pity to break up the Easter Liturgy as experienced as a single entity by our spiritual forebears, and the aim should be wherever possible to maintain the unity of the whole rite, prolonged though it may be.

Sequential options

Common Worship: Times and Seasons (2006) provides two alternative approaches to the celebration of the Easter Liturgy as a composite rite incorporating all four segments: *Pattern A*, which begins with the Service of Light leading into the Vigil, followed by the Liturgies of Initiation and the Eucharist; and *Pattern B*, which reverses the first two segments, with a lengthier and more reflective Vigil leading into a Service of Light at cock-crow. The Liturgies of Initiation and the Eucharist then follow as in Pattern A. The mood and setting of the Vigil in Pattern B is that of storytelling round a campfire, and lends itself to a more 'adventurous and creative approach'.

Pattern B challenges the ancient tradition of the Service of Light followed by the Vigil, and quite rightly so. It is one of those traditions which we enter into automatically as the unquestioned way in which things are done. In the cold light of day it is of course illogical, for surely the faithful longing of the Hebrew people commemorated in the Vigil should culminate, not begin, with the breaking through of the light of Christ. *Times and Seasons* does the Church great service in allowing us to consider these questions which may well end in the disruption of our time-honoured routines.

Pattern B also requires that we take a little more time and trouble than usual to move out of our habitual patterns of worship, in which we can drive largely on automatic, and to strike out in some new directions. For example, in this scenario the Vigil is experienced more as a preparatory service in its own right than the first part of an Easter celebration that rolls inexorably forward. The Vigil may even last all night, and will involve participants in a grappling with the significance of the stories from the Scriptures, rather than closing down our minds in order to get onto the next section.

If we take the Pattern B approach to the Vigil, therefore, the venue should certainly be a place other than the liturgical space where the rest of the Easter Liturgy is to happen. It may be outside, around a small bonfire, or at least begin outside before moving into a suitable building, for example a church hall, for the Vigil proper. The lighting of a fire will set off the proceedings, but at this point it is a fire to focus the gathering and to provide light for the readers and storytellers to read by, not the New Fire of the Service of Light, which will come later (though the mood of the Vigil in Pattern B is deliberately so tentative and uncertain, full of longing and expectation, that one is never sure what will happen next).

The Vigil in this setting will be much more free and easy and exploratory. The readings from the Scriptures may well be dramatized, or retold in our own words.

If we truly mean business about celebrating the Easter Liturgy in a way which allows us to enter into the spirit of the early Church's experience, then whichever pattern we adopt, the essential thing is to fix the time of the Liturgy to ensure that we begin in the dark but end in the light. The time will vary according to the date of Easter and of when summertime begins. Usually 5.00 a.m. will be found to work, and although some years it may be possible to make it a little later, it is probably best to stick to the same time every year at an hour that works. It is not the best of starts to go to all this trouble and find the first rays of the sun illuminating the Easter fire; in this situation it's a case of better early than never.

Choreography

The Easter Liturgy as set out below follows the traditional order of Light–Vigil–Initiation–Eucharist, but the alternative, and in many ways more logical, sequence of Vigil–Light–Initiation–Eucharist (commended in Pattern B of *Common Worship: Times and Seasons*) will not be lost sight of.

The Service of Light

The Service of Light: blessing the New Fire

The assembly gathers in the churchyard or garden alongside or in close proximity to the place of liturgical celebration. Here on the previous day a small bonfire has been laid (an activity which children usually enjoy participating in). In some locations this will need to be guarded, or to be brought out at the last minute, human nature being what it is.

Although there is a school of thought that the New Fire should be kindled at the beginning of the liturgy by some suitably quaint method involving flint or boy scouts rubbing sticks together, this vastly increases the risk of what the late Wilfred Pickles called 'an embarrassing moment'. Furthermore, nothing can beat a blazing, crackling fire as a gathering point for a crowd on a dark and drizzly morning before first light.

Here is the campfire around which the community can gather and tell stories about its history and journey to this place and time. Traditionally this fire is the New Fire blessed at the outset by the president, but it can serve equally well as the fire around which the stories of the Vigil will be told and chewed over before moving on later to bless the New Fire and light the Easter Candle.

Assuming however that the traditional sequence will be followed, members of the assembly are handed on arrival both the orders of service and the individual tapers which will be lit from the Paschal Candle as soon as it is blessed, lit and carried into the liturgical space.

At the appointed hour the president and other liturgical ministers emerge quietly from the church building and join the rest of the assembly at the fire. The president first blesses the New Fire and censes it. Then the deacon, or other minister, steps forward holding the Paschal Candle which is then inscribed by the president, using the beautiful words from the Book of Revelation pertaining to Christ the 'Alpha and Omega'. Five symbolic incense studs (made of some synthetic material) are then inserted into the candle at the points and centre of the cross, as the president proclaims these deeply resonant words:

By his holy
and glorious wounds
may Christ our Lord
guard us
and keep us.

The Paschal Candle is then lit from the New Fire, which is often easier said than done. The first hazard is that any attempt to light a taper from the fire results usually in a very sad-looking melted taper rather than a living flame. Something like a slender splinter of wood is needed to catch a light from the fire, which can then be transferred to the taper and then to the candle. The second hazard is that the slightest breeze will wreak havoc with the enterprise. It is good to practise these things without a crowd looking on, and to have back-up in the form of a server with a concealed weapon such as a cigarette lighter.

Once the Paschal Candle is lit, the deacon lifts it high and leads the way into the place where the Vigil is to be celebrated, the server with cigarette lighter sticking in close, but discreet, attendance. Upon entering the liturgical space the deacon begins the threefold acclamation of the Paschal Candle at three stations between the entrance and the Paschal Candle stand.

Timing is everything. As in most liturgical situations, the most common fault is being in too much of a hurry. It is essential that a sufficient proportion of the assembly has also entered the building and has gathered round the candle before the deacon first proclaims 'The Light of Christ!' A goodly crowd is necessary to make a sufficiently hearty response of 'Thanks be to God' and to sound as if they mean it. A significant amount of time (always more than you think) is then needed to allow members of the assembly to have their hand-held candles lit from the Paschal Candle.

Because the deacon carrying the Paschal Candle is in no position to peer round and check out things for herself, this is a moment when an experienced Master of

Ceremonies will be worth his weight in gold. Those responsible for an act of worship as complex as the Easter Vigil all need to look to one person who knows exactly what comes next and who does what; that person's word is law! Clued-up ushers ready to go, tapers in hand, are also pearls without price on these occasions.

The deacon should not set out for the second station until the majority of those gathered at the first station have their tapers lit, and so at the second station where again a significant amount of time needs to be given to the process of spreading the light to the individual tapers and so throughout the whole liturgical space. As we give and receive light from one another, a single voice might sound out in the darkness the Iona chant:

> Kindle a flame to lighten the dark
>   And take all fear away.

This is then taken up by all, at first softly and hesitantly, but with growing confidence and joy.

Having arrived at the third station, and sung the final acclamation, the deacon places the Paschal Candle in the stand prepared for it. The candle is then censed by the deacon.

On this holy night the Paschal Candle stand should take centre stage in the middle of the liturgical space. Later, for the rest of Eastertide, when it is lit at every liturgy, it can be placed near the ambo where Christ the living Word is proclaimed. Outside the Easter season, when it is lit only for rites of initiation, it stands by the baptismal font. The common practice of parking the Paschal Candle near the high altar, together with other bits of furniture no one quite knows what to do with, has neither rhyme nor reason.

The stand holding the candle needs to be substantial and robust, not flimsy, or inconsequential, or easily knocked over. A thorough search of the church basement, or of local used-furniture shops, is often rewarded with a suitable piece of furniture which can be adapted or cannibalized to make a stand of sufficient presence in the space. The material is of secondary importance to its stature. Wood or brass are usually the best, wrought iron in this instance never looking quite up to the seriousness of the job. If all else fails, an enquiry to a maker of theatre props may yield better results than a trawl of the ecclesiastical catalogues.

It is customary to decorate the rim of the Paschal Candle stand with small spring flowers, but over-enthusiasm on the part of the flower arrangers needs to be watched. An essential pastoral skill not taught at theological college is the ability to keep the flower arrangers happy while harnessing their gifts to the liturgical needs of the day. In this case, the deacon should not have to stumble through dense undergrowth in order to place or retrieve the Paschal Candle during the Vigil. Understatement always says the most.

The Paschal Candle having been placed in its central position and censed, the deacon goes to the ambo to sing the Exsultet, the ancient hymn of praise to the new light of Easter. The text usually sung today dates from around the eighth century, and its chant is considered one of the finest examples extant from that period. Here singing should trump holy orders, and if the deacon has no voice, a cantor should stand alongside the deacon and sing the proclamation for the benefit of the whole assembly. This is too important a moment to fall foul of restrictive practices.

It should be remembered, however, that originally the deacon would have composed his own proclamation of praise, as would the president a eucharistic prayer. In places where the local assembly exhibits the necessary gifts and talents, there is no reason why the ancient custom should not be revived and a new proclamation created for the occasion. As with flower arrangers and banner-makers, however, the pastor needs to hone the skill of being able to say 'no' when appropriate.

Common Worship: Times and Seasons (2006) provides several interesting alternatives for the Exsultet, including a responsorial version, a metrical version and a modern translation (see pp. 410–17). This is a timely reminder that it is the purpose of the Exsultet, rather than its particular text or chant, that is the essential thing. To hear the traditional Exsultet sung with expertise and panache is a spine-tingling moment but, no matter how inspiring, one can be left with a feeling of exclusion; that the assembly was deprived of a chance to express in song its own joyful response to the light that has pierced its darkness.

In matters liturgical it is usually possible to have the best of both worlds, and the option on page 410 of *Common Worship: Times and Seasons* (2006) suggests one way forward, that of substituting a metrical version of the Introduction sung by the people, for the traditional one sung by the deacon or minister alone. Alternatively, at the end of the Exsultet, the assembly could burst forth in response with a song such as Kathleen Thomerson's 'I want to walk as a child of the light' (*The Hymnal 1982*, no. 490) to the tune 'Houston'.

Following the singing of the proclamation, the deacon and other ministers go to their places alongside the president.

The Vigil

The president greets the people and intones the prayer of the day, and the assembly is then seated. Everything is now ready for the Easter Liturgy to enter its next phase: the Vigil readings.

At this point the assembly has a moment to look round and take stock of its surroundings. The beauty of the Easter Vigil is that in candlelight any brute of a building will begin to look half alluring, but this requires of us a seriousness about the movement from darkness into light; no cheating!

All kinds of reasons may be produced for having some artificial light in place to supplement the hand candles (there's always a health and safety type lurking in the shadows to spoil the fun), but these should be resisted at all costs. The whole point of the Vigil is the glory of the light of Christ penetrating and transforming the darkness, but to grasp this, the darkness from which we emerge needs to be total and complete. Some concession may be made for the musician who may need a small lamp over the keyboard, but the rest of us must stumble along hopefully, our candle piercing the dark.

The place of celebration of the Easter Liturgy is, for the majority of faith communities, the same place as that in which we meet week by week, day by day. This however should not dissuade us from exploring other possibilities (such as a crypt or undercroft) as a venue for the Vigil before moving into the main space for the rest of the Easter Liturgy. Such spaces may have low headroom or be restricted in other ways, which make them of little general use, but they can come into their own when we need a space to recall for us the catacombs of the early Christians.

When we stick with the main liturgical space for the whole of the Easter Liturgy, however, the same room that we inhabit week after week, the challenge for us is to so transform the space that it is hardly recognizable. The liturgical space thereby becomes in itself a parable of our new life in the Risen Christ, of our passing from utter darkness into glorious, blinding light.

This requires imagination and hard work in the limited time frame of Holy Saturday, but it is a good opportunity to give to the frustrated interior designers among us their head (but, knowing interior designers, a budget will be a wise move). Even the dullest of interiors can be transformed by hangings and by lighting and other tricks of the trade.

To awake on Easter morning to a new world embodied by a barely recognizable liturgical space with a high 'wow!' factor will help lift our liturgy to a new plane. It was said of James Wilson (Residentiary Canon of Worcester 1905–26) that he 'woke every morning to a new world' (Beeson, 2006). That's a fine epitaph for any Christian; let it be said of us on Easter morning at least.

In the Vigil, this transformed interior will only gradually become apparent, as the dawn slowly breaks in upon our Easter rites of recalling and rejoicing. At first, the only light will be that shed by the candles held by each of the faithful, and this should continue throughout the readings from the Hebrew Scriptures. Thereafter we shall move into a different phase, as both artificial light and natural light from outside combine to lift our spirits as we soar into the New Covenant of the Risen Lord.

But first we continue in the darkness, clutching our candles around the great candle which is Christ's new light, and recall the long search of God's people for meaning and direction and hope. This great and solemn Liturgy of the Word is an important piece of our spiritual formation, and should not be rushed through in order to get to the 'interesting bits' of the resurrection story, let alone the champagne breakfast.

We have to be realistic in assessing just how much of the Judaeo-Christian pilgrimage of faith has sunk in for the average member of a faith community today. It is highly probable, almost a certainty, that the Easter Vigil is the only opportunity in the whole year for the average member to listen to a comprehensive summary of our salvation story. Here is a rare chance for the connections to be made and the parallels brought to the fore; we must seize it with both hands. How might we do this?

First the pace of the Liturgy of the Word should be slowed down, to walking rather than running pace. The bearing of the president; the manner in which the readings are introduced and briefly explained; the trouble taken to make each reading as dramatic and arresting as possible, with at least two voices for those readings involving dialogue; the silences after each reading; the choice of music to bring alive the psalm after each reading; all these factors will play a part in making the Liturgy of the Word an engaging and edifying experience rather than an ordeal to be sat through stoically.

Silence will have a particular place in our experience of making Vigil, given a vigil's primary characteristic of watchful waiting. At the regular Sunday assembly we have to fight for a place for silence as integral to liturgical life, for our worship is all too often a headlong dash from one bit of chatter to the next. At the Easter Vigil we can deliberately slow our liturgical metabolism right down, making ourselves fully aware of the moment in which, alert and at peace with ourselves, we are enabled to appreciate afresh the anointing of God.

A decision which has a great bearing on the pace and rhythm of the Liturgy of the Word is of course that concerning the number of readings to be included. Whereas the American *Book of Common Prayer* (1979) provides nine readings, *Common Worship: Times and Seasons* (2006) provides no less than twenty-two. Over and above the foundational story of Israel's deliverance at the Red Sea, Exodus 14.10—15.1, which is mandatory, there is a growing choice of readings available.

When the Vigil is planned to go right through the night, then all twenty-two readings, interspersed with silence and music, will come in handy. For most purposes, however, some process of selection must be entered into.

If we are intent on making the Vigil as meaningful as possible, then a careful pastoral decision to achieve a sensible number of readings will be essential. Better to have five or six readings well presented at a moderate pace than nine or ten rushed through at a rattling fast speed without pause for breath. Remember, this is not a liturgical marathon but a once-a-year opportunity for Christian formation. What matters above all is that people *hear* the story, and in the words of the old Prayer Book collect, also 'mark, learn and inwardly digest' what they have heard, taking it deeply into themselves.

To this end also it may be necessary to think the unthinkable and apply some common sense to the length and content of the passages selected. We need of course hefty chunks of Scripture set before us, but when eyes begin to glaze over and people to shuffle in their seats, we shall know that our public Bible reading shows valour rather than discretion. This would not go down too well in some circles, but for those not averse to this suggestion, abbreviated forms of one or two of the longer and more repetitive readings are suggested in Appendix 2.

In addition, it would be no bad thing to add other readings from non-scriptural sources, for example a reading on the theme of deliverance. This might take the form of a description of God's blessing or of humankind's rising above itself in sacrificial love, whether in a Sudanese refugee camp, or in New York on 9/11, or at a roadside in Iraq.

Before the readings begin, the president should explain what is going to happen, and the purpose of the exercise: that amidst our frantic activity of getting and spending, this ancient rite of the Church bids us stop and recall God's overarching love and provision, and the yearning of humanity for the God without whom we are consigned to hopelessness.

Each reading should be introduced by the president, or other minister, or by the reader if guided and prepared, so that the assembly does not suddenly find itself catapulted into a lengthy section of the Hebrew Scriptures of little seeming relevance to their current situation.

The Vigil has a rhythm all of its own, in which both silence and music play a crucial role. The periods of silence after each reading should be controlled by the president, who after each period will then call upon the assembly to rise, and pray the collect appropriate to each reading.

Before each collect, there is provided in Pattern A of *Common Worship: Times and Seasons* (2006) an inspired set of christological responses, said by president and assembly, which root the readings from the Hebrew Scriptures in the hope and expectation of the Church. The readings are read by the light of the Easter Candle, and understood in the light of Christ.

The choice of music is of huge importance in complementing the readings and giving the whole Vigil a sense of expectation, longing and joy. Churning out the old familiar stuff simply will not do. It is helpful if in the Vigil we can ring the changes between the different ways in which we can sing the psalms – contemporary responsorial perhaps alternating with versions in which the singers do their thing on our behalf. A typical programme of blended psalmody for the Vigil, using several different sources, is found at the end of this section.

When all the Vigil readings with accompanying psalms and prayers are concluded, our Easter morning rites enter a dramatic new phase. Where the Service of Light has not taken place earlier, this is the moment when the Easter Candle is carried by the deacon with great joy and anticipation into the midst of the assembly. The ceremonies honouring the candle and the singing of the Exsultet would now follow.

Where the traditional sequence is followed, there is at the conclusion of the Vigil an equally dramatic change in mood and tempo, and the signal for this is the proclamation of the Easter Acclamation. In reply to the president's 'Alleluia. Christ is Risen', the assembly shouts 'He is risen indeed. Alleluia, alleluia, alleluia'. This may be repeated, several times if so desired, with gradually increasing volume.

It is absolutely vital that the Easter Acclamation does not fall flat on its face. Although it may seem more ambitious and even risky to sing rather than say the Easter Acclamation, it does at least mean that there is a group of people who have rehearsed their lines and know their cue, ready to crash in with gusto. The setting may be simple or complex, but as long as it is done with panache all shall be well. The said (or rather shouted) version is fine too, but needs to be an instant and roaring response; a split second hesitation or less than tumultuous roar will rob the moment of its power, and it is one of those things one cannot practise without spoiling the surprise.

The Easter Acclamation gives birth immediately to a cacophony of sound appropriate to a 'riotous assembly' of joyful Christians ready to party after a time of austerity. The people of God now let rip with their weird and wonderful collection of things with which to make a merry noise.

This is a telling moment for the parish priest, at which the goats are separated from the sheep. Most of us remember the need to ask the assembly to come equipped with bells and whistles about one minute before we are about to sing the Gloria. Instead, we need to have this all sorted weeks in advance, and this requires a Holy Week checklist reminding all concerned of what is required to be in place by when.

This should be a great moment for the assembly, especially for the kids; a rare moment when children of all ages are invited to make as much noise in worship as they can muster. Bells of various kinds are a good start, but horns, rattles and even saucepan lids will do nicely also. It is also good to track down some fun things from manufacturers of trivial 'novelties'. One year at Philadelphia, everyone found in their place a pair of plastic hands which when shaken produced a clapping sound; it was difficult to get them to stop.

After a few moments, while the joyful sound continues, a fanfare announces the *Gloria in Excelsis Deo*. Most often this will be played on the organ, but if there is any doubt about the organist's ability to deliver the goods, drums, percussion or brass will of course do the job equally well, if not better.

The Gloria, the song of praise we trundle out at most Sunday Liturgies in the year (except penitential seasons), on this occasion assumes a fresh and startling significance, for on this day it ushers in our new dawn, as we emerge from a long night into Christ's glorious day.

Care needs to be taken here to combine the familiar with the outrageously different. The setting needs to be totally familiar to the assembly, so that no one has to *think* but simply sing, especially if the cacophony of sound made by the people continues throughout. The difference lies in the introduction and the stage management. It is very important indeed that this moment should not be an anti-climax but, to ensure this, careful preparation is required.

At the same time the lights in the liturgical space are brought up to full blast, and if there isn't much blast to be had, temporary lighting to highlight the focal points (try the local dramatic society) should supplement the usual glimmer. This is the moment when hand candles are extinguished.

The Liturgy of the Eucharist, framing the Liturgy of Initiation, now begins in earnest as the president greets the people and intones the Prayer of the Day. The first reading from the Christian Scriptures then follows, that from St Paul's letter to the church in Rome. The mood has changed, the light has dawned, and the reader needs to reflect this in bearing as well as manner of declamation. The process by which readers are chosen and trained will reveal much about the liturgical priorities of the pastor.

After the reading from Romans comes the Alleluia. Here again, as with the Gloria, of paramount importance is the ability of the assembly to join in, rather than that of a choir to show off. The traditional Alleluia is simple enough. Provided the deacon is confident, the assembly can be confident in repeating what has been sung. It should be a shout of praise of the whole assembly; the need for a joyous (even raucous) response trumping that for a series of correct notes.

Common Worship: Times and Seasons (2006) provides a fourfold alternative to the traditional scriptural sentence and Alleluia, in which four short scriptural phrases on the resurrection theme are responded to by the assembly with 'Alleluia'. Given an able deacon, this rather staccato version delivered with sonority will be extremely effective.

The deacon, or other designated liturgical minister, then proceeds to the ambo to cense the Gospel Book and then sing the Gospel. This is definitely a day for singing rather than reading, and as with the Exsultet, if the deacon is unsure of singing, let another take the deacon's place. This is no time for standing on ceremony, for the good news must be proclaimed from the housetop, as beautifully and as powerfully as we can.

The Gospel having been proclaimed, the assembly is seated for the homily. As on so many occasions during Holy Week, the preached word is almost superfluous if we have got the liturgy right. Nevertheless we usually feel obliged to add a word or two, but that's what it should be; an economical drawing out from the liturgy a word which will encourage or convince or mobilize. This is one of those occasions when the fewer the words the more telling the message.

After the homily, a period of silence follows, in which we can begin to digest all that we have done so far in this journeying celebration.

The Liturgy of Initiation

Liturgy of Initiation: the presentation of the candidates

After the silence, the assembly is invited into the next phase of the Easter celebration: the rite of Christian initiation. (This moment in the Easter Liturgy brings into focus a couple of particular issues – Christian formation and liturgical design. These are addressed in the boxes below.)

Christian formation

Local circumstances may make it difficult to drum up candidates every year, but no stone should be left unturned, or hedgerow undisturbed, in the search for those who will, in the context of the Great Vigil of Easter, mark publicly the irruption of the grace of God in their lives.

We are not talking here of course of persuading the reluctant on a last-minute 'Oh why not?' basis, but of a year-long attentiveness to the nurturing of those responsible adults who seek God in their lives and who are open to placing themselves at the disposal of God and of the community of fellow seekers, the Church. This is to understand Christian initiation as process, not event.

This process is 'year-long' because always at the back of our mind should be desirability of shepherding new catechumens into a schedule of formation which leads into an intensive Lenten training programme culminating in their admission at the Easter Vigil. It is also restricted to 'responsible adults' simply because the Church has for too long, by attempting to herd into membership flocks of giggling younger teenagers, devalued the currency of belonging and invited a high lapse rate. By reviving the practice at least in outline of the early Church in both preparation and initiation, there is a better chance of the whole business being taken seriously and a change of direction in life effected.

To achieve a reawakened sense of Christian initiation in the context of life-long formation, a number of things need to happen. The annual schedule of training and preparation for membership should be geared to the Easter Liturgy, so that the process by which candidates for initiation are discerned and encouraged and trained is designed to 'come to the boil' through Lent, with Easter as the culmination of the community of faith's journey.

This is easier said than done; parents desiring baptism for their infant children are often loath to delay the event, and can be initially dumbfounded at the very notion of a 5 a.m. start on a late March morning. However, these should be seen merely as teething troubles. At least Easter, being a holiday weekend, is a time when most godparents and relatives are available (unlike the rest of the year when limited availability is used as an excuse to demand a baptism date inconvenient to all but the family). If we persist, then slowly the word spreads and the Easter Liturgy is experienced rather than imagined, and the whole thing begins to take root in the life of a parish.

In a parish of any size baptisms will obviously need to take place at several times throughout a typical year, but the pastor with half an eye cast on liturgical formation will always strive to keep a few candidates up his/her sleeve for the Big Day. Certainly the concept of a baptism at the Easter Vigil will gain increasing appeal among committed church families the more it is experienced in the flesh of an Easter morning.

With confirmation it is usually a little easier to control and direct the flow of candidates towards an Easter event, and in the early days at least (before every parish wants to get in line!) it is going to take an imaginative bishop to claim he already has something in his diary at 5 a.m. on Easter Day. Bishops should be fairly easy game to capture for an Easter Liturgy at this time, and might even enjoy it so much that they urge it upon others.

If so, this obviously ensures an even more festive dimension to the Vigil, with attendant friends and family members cheering on the candidates. Needless to say we are speaking here of confirmation candidates of reasonable age, that is, of an age when they will be making other important decisions in their lives about careers and relationships. They should be able to string a word or two together, and not giggle and nudge their way through the proceedings.

Liturgical design

To this end, the redesign of baptismal fonts (dealt with in more detail in my *Re-Pitching the Tent*) achieves an importance which is pastoral as much as architectural. We cannot seriously expect those entering into a full experience of the Christian faith to make a connection between 'rebirth through the waters of baptism' and a bird bath standing unused in a corner of the south transept.

Existing fonts need to be dragged screaming out of their corners and cubbyholes into the full light of day, to be relocated in a place where they cannot be missed, either at the entrance into the liturgical space or in a spacious setting in their own right where the assembly can gather around them. Note that this precludes always and everywhere the retrograde step of placing the font (in the interests of 'visibility') up front on the liturgical 'stage' alongside altar and lectern, a practice which effectively puts the clock back in our liturgical understanding by several generations.

All font lids and canopies, no matter how valuable or interesting or historical, need to be consigned to the museum, the junk shop or the council tip, unless they are sufficiently grand to justify being permanently suspended high above the font.

Fonts should be filled with water at all times, irrespective of whether a baptism is in the offing or not. The water needs to be seen to be overflowing and splashing everywhere, as a sign of God's abundant and unstinting grace, and, furthermore, energy, ingenuity and financial investment should be allocated to come up with some solution incorporating a pool alongside the existing font, with water continually circulating between them.

If the existing font is uncooperative, or leaks, or is just plain ugly, then it should be sacrificed for the greater good of our communal future, and replaced. It may often be the case that we need to start all over again with something entirely new which speaks more fittingly and eloquently of our reawakened understanding of baptismal life, and we should not be squeamish or sentimental when this is required of us.

Hopefully, then, the assembly can move in joyful procession at the Easter Vigil from the ministry of the word to the rites of initiation. Appropriate music should accompany and lift this movement of expectancy and hope. As we crowd around the baptismal pool, the younger ones weaving between our legs, peeping round, to get a better view, we live out humankind's fascination with, yet fear of, that water in which we might drown but without which we cannot hope to live. Like the fountain in the town square on a sweltering day, the font draws us and centres us.

As we have seen, it is essential at the regular Sunday Liturgy that the assembly gathers at the font irrespective of whether or not a baptism is to take place. We need to weave this element of Christian worship into the very fabric of our weekly assembly. How much more so at the Easter Liturgy!

The president invites the assembly to process to the font, and on its way the assembly should sing; it's what we do when we march and when we are confident of victory. Singing on a journey should be simple and repetitive, something that can be immediately picked up aurally, allowing us to dispense with leaflets or books.

There is a lot to be said for singing at this point a litany of the saints, provided we can focus on the companionship in prayer of our illustrious forebears rather than on any superstitious vanity in which saints become objects of prayer rather than fellow Christians who pray alongside us. Provided we get this straight, it is a good and godly thing to sing the catechumens to the baptismal waters with the names of the heroes of our faith – the martyrs, the confessors and all holy men and women – ringing in our ears.

There are some very fine contemporary settings of the Litany of the Saints, though as good Anglicans we may have to indulge in a little judicious pruning here and there of the more fanciful or politicized candidates for canonization who over time have sneaked into the heavenly courts via the back door. It is also good to give more prominent place to saints of our region or to those associated with our faith community. In the United States, for example, a part of the world a little short on fully paid-up saints of the calendar, it is a wonderful thing to mention Jonathan Daniels, a seminarian murdered in 1965 in Alabama during the Civil Rights Movement, alongside Maximilian Kolbe, George Herbert, Julian of Norwich, Chad and Cuthbert.

At the font, the assembly gathers around, crowding in untidily and uncontrollably but entirely appropriately. This is a time for standing on chairs or sitting on window sills to get a good view, in the spirit of Eutychus (Acts 20.9–12) but without the dramatic grand finale.

The president begins the Liturgy of Initiation by asking the candidates to come forward, accompanied by their sponsors. There is a nice touch in *Common Worship: Times and Seasons* (2006) where it suggests that, where possible, baptismal candidates should not enter the liturgical space beyond the font until the Liturgy of Initiation begins. This recalls the ancient practice by which the catechumens were excluded from the eucharistic assembly, and helps to up the liturgical ante. Where the font is near the entrance this obviously works within a natural progression, but where the font is more centrally placed the candidates could remain in their places near the entrance until summoned forth by the president, like Lazarus from the grave, at the beginning of the Liturgy of Initiation.

The role of sponsor, while not absolutely essential, is a ministry to be encouraged and lionized. A sponsor should be a member of the assembly into which the candidate is being received; a person who perhaps befriended them when they first arrived, or nurtured them as they went along. It is a noble calling, and one greatly blessed, to play Ananias to the candidate's Paul (Acts 9.10–19).

The initial question to the candidate establishing his/her desire to go forward is a simple, no-nonsense question, and opportunity is then given here for testimony. This is to be applauded for many reasons: first, it signifies our movement into a new era of serious adult discipleship rather than adolescent going-through-the-motions; second, it shows that mainstream Christianity may just be willing to learn from other traditions in which the giving of testimony is one of the main planks of Christian formation whereby members of the assembly learn from one another and the Body of Christ is built up.

The Decision then follows, the words of which are used, in the absence of baptismal candidates, for the Re-affirmation of Baptismal Vows by the whole assembly. In that case, the people may be invited here to relight their individual candles, and also again at the Commission and Sending Out at the very end of the Easter Liturgy.

At the risk of sounding unduly pragmatic, however, the relighting and then the extinguishing of candles at these points, although in theory highly symbolic, can become something of a palaver which even in the best run circles tends to bring the liturgy to a grinding halt. Having given the hand candles a good run for their money throughout the Vigil, it is probably best on balance just to give in gracefully to artificial light once the house lights have been brought up at the Gloria. If there is to be relighting of hand candles, the less disruptive moment is probably at the final Sending Out, but by that time hopefully sunlight is streaming in, and the gesture may seem a little academic.

The candidates now renounce their old life and then affirm their new. The words of what we now call the Decision have ebbed and flowed over the centuries. The Book of Common Prayer (1662) required of candidates (or those speaking for them) that they 'renounce the devil and all his works', for in keeping with the tradition of the Western Church, baptism was seen primarily as a washing away of that original sin which Augustine of Hippo so unhelpfully went on about.

By the time of the *Alternative Service Book 1980*, there was widespread dissatisfaction with the notion of imputing sins to infants, and the words of the Decision reflect this. The single question is replaced by a threefold formula covering intention, repentance and renunciation. The questions are short, sharp and simple, and although repentance is still a primary element (the same formula is used for adults), the phraseology is open to a wider interpretation of the remission of sins in baptism. Furthermore the devil was sent packing, or at least cut out of the script.

Common Worship: Christian Initiation (2006) sets out to break new ground, setting baptism firmly in the lifelong process of Christian formation. It makes even more explicit the expectation that baptism will take place within the context of Sunday public worship, and will be understood in the context of an ongoing baptismal life in the community of faith. Material is provided to anchor the baptismal rite in the liturgical year, in which Easter is seen as of primary significance.

The Decision is longer and wordier, now containing six questions, three dealing with the past (rejection, renunciation and repentance) and three with the future (turning, submitting, coming to Christ), but they are clear and direct. Although the devil makes a reappearance, it is within the context of that 'rebellion against God' which afflicts us all, and repentance is likewise set in the context of the common human experience of separation.

The threefold decision from the *Alternative Services Book 1980* (now appearing somewhat staccato) are retained as an alternative tucked away in a back page for use 'when there are strong pastoral reasons'. These reasons are not specified, and give rise to much speculation on the part of those of an inventive imagination. Do the pastoral reasons suggest the emergence of an Alternative Service Book lobbying group to counter the baleful influence of the Prayer Book Society?

In general the affirmations concerning the new life in Christ desired by the candidate have been made sharper and more personal. The notion of submitting to Christ, rather than having a sneaking regard for him, is a significant step forward towards the whole event being taken seriously by all concerned.

The water is then blessed, which at the Easter Vigil means a great deal more than setting aside some water in a bowl for a particular ceremony. Here we are symbolically blessing the water supply for a whole year, a fact that will make more sense to us when we are gathered around a baptismal pool with flowing water central to the liturgical space rather than a bird bath in the corner. The blessing of water at subsequent baptisms throughout the year is therefore superfluous, until such time as the water is evidently past its sell-by date (when you see dead mice floating in it, you know its time for a change).

The responsorial form of blessing provided in *Common Worship: Times and Seasons* (2006, p. 343) is excellent, not only because it breaks up the fairly long traditional recitation of the ways water has been used in the story of God's rescue mission to humankind, but also because the first line of the response, 'Saving God', can be said by the deacon or other minister, the assembly responding with the second line, 'give us life'.

The problem with responses interjected into a long prayer is always that of the cueing in the response. Unless this is crystal clear, any attempt to pray thoughtfully is undone by anxiety about when exactly to pipe up with our response. A two-part response as indicated here overcomes that problem admirably, provided the deacon stays awake.

It is customary for the Easter Candle to be lowered into the water during this blessing, as a sign of the baptism into Christ's death that we may also be raised with him. In the new prayer this would most fittingly take place during the fourth petition at the mention of our being 'made one with Christ in his death'. Some women colleagues give disapproving glances at this point, but I think this may refer to something my mummy never told me about.

The Profession of Faith follows, said by all, including candidates for initiation when present. The form suggested is the responsorial version of the Apostles' Creed, which is a good enough version and superior, in its basic simplicity and economy, to the more theologically long-winded Nicene Creed served up to us most Sunday mornings. Even more appropriate perhaps at the Easter Liturgy might be the use of a three-fold baptismal formula, in accordance with ancient practice prior to political theologians getting in on the act. The rubrics allow for this when there are 'strong pastoral reasons' for doing so, and protecting the people of God from the need of experts to complicate the good news of Jesus Christ should be a solemn duty of the ordained.

The transition from the corporate profession of faith on the part of the whole assembly to the individual candidate's own personal affirmation is achieved beautifully by the president's question to the candidate(s) immediately following the creedal affirmation by the people.

Using the candidate's name (for 'I have called you by name, you are mine', Isaiah 43.1), the president asks of the candidate whether they too can lay claim to the faith just professed by the assembly:

N. is this your faith?

In response, the candidate may either repeat the phrase in the affirmative or answer in his/her own words.

This is something of a breakthrough in Anglican liturgical usage, but completely at one with ancient practice in which the liturgical forms provided merely the framework for extempore prayer. This approach was in the Early Church not confined to a catechumen's response to a simple question, but included even the president's offering of the eucharistic prayer. Over time our responses and prayers have become formalized and ritualized, robbing us of spontaneity and even at times of a sense of serious and sincere intent. If you doubt this, count the seconds between a question asked by a bishop at a confirmation and the mumbled embarrassed reply.

The president then proceeds to baptize the candidate, dipping infant candidates in the water, or pouring water over those who are children or adults.

Immediately after the baptism, the candidates are led into a side room or sacristy to be clothed in an alb as a sign of their new life.

Clothing

The option of reviving the ancient custom of clothing the newly baptized in a white garment, to which *Common Worship: Times and Seasons* (2006) recalls us, should be seized with both hands. An alb may conveniently be used for the clothing, accompanied by the pronouncement of words from that rich vein of Scripture in which the new life enjoyed by the follower of Jesus the Christ is likened to being fitted out with a new suit of clothes (Galatians 3.27):

You have been clothed with Christ
As many as are baptized into Christ have put on Christ

This restoration of the ancient practice of clothing the newly baptized is a huge step forward, transforming what was (if it was done at all) an eccentricity on the part of the parish priest to a ritual act of primitive authenticity redolent of transformation and new life.

Being clothed anew is a powerful sign of second birth that resonates again and again through the Christian Scriptures. Those who are clothed in the baptismal garment do so in order that we may 'put on the Lord Jesus Christ' (Romans 13.14) and be counted among the 'great multitude that no one could count' (Revelation

7.9) 'from every nation, from all tribes and peoples and languages, standing before the throne and before the Lamb, clothed in white robes, with palm branches in their hands'. It is ironic to note that in stripping our liturgies of symbolic ritual and gesture, the Reformers deprived us for over four hundred years of forceful ways in which to bring Scripture alive in our own experience. Their restoration is to be applauded and the resultant opportunities embraced.

While they are being dried off and reclothed, it is the turn of the whole assembly to get wet, as the people are sprinkled.

The liturgy therefore continues in tactile mode as the assembly is now brought into contact with the baptismal waters, no longer merely a theological abstract but real wet stuff. This can be encountered either corporately, the president sprinkling the assembly with water from the font; or individually, each member of the assembly being invited to step forward to dip the tip of a finger in the water and to sign themselves (or better still their neighbour), with the sign of the cross on their forehead. In either case, a song in celebration of the waters of new life (and we are spoiled for choice here) should always accompany this rite.

Once again, what was formerly the rarified preserve of the few (that is, parishes considered 'full faith') is now the common possession of the many, and potentially of all. Old prejudices may die hard, but we should never allow them to spoil a good liturgical party.

After the sprinkling, the candidates rejoin the community at the font or in the middle of the liturgical space. Here they are signed with the sign of the cross on their foreheads. In *Common Worship: Christian Initiation* (2006) this is the secondary option, the first being to do the signing earlier in the rite, before baptism and immediately after the profession of faith. The later point assumed here seems more natural and more theological, 'sealing the Spirit' with oil.

Although this 'branding' of the flock of Christ is performed usually by the president, the rubrics here contain a flash of inspiration when they suggest that the sponsor might do so.

It seems that this is proposed as an additional signing, but there is no reason why the sponsor should not be the sole signer on behalf of the whole community, in true Ananias mode. The sponsor alone could say the words:

Christ claims you for his own
Receive the sign of the cross

and then the president would chime in with the words:

Do not be ashamed to confess the faith of Christ crucified

which is the cue for the whole assembly to raise the swell of mutual encouragement in the life of discipleship:

Fight valiantly as a disciple of Christ
against sin, the world and the devil,
and remain faithful to Christ to the end of your life.

Holy oil should be used for the signing, simply because it is the most natural thing in the world and of course deeply scriptural. The fact that it is not mentioned in the rubrics is a sure sign of a committee at work. No doubt someone had a Protestant hang-up about oil which has deprived us at this point of the full richness of the rite. We can but rise up in rebellion against such illogicality and contrariness, and anoint away, liberally and joyously.

The president then says the prayer of reception over the newly baptized, and the assembly greets them with applause (if there are Confirmations, the greeting and applause will be at the conclusion of both rites).

If Confirmations are to take place, then this is the moment, and it is entirely appropriate for the bishop to administer the laying on of hands at the font also, avoiding any tedious movement back to the chair. The candidates for Confirmation, having already been baptized and therefore eligible to wear the baptismal garment, will have been clothed in albs for the whole of the Vigil.

There now follows the Commission: the rallying call to those newly initiated into the full Christian life to know and to remember who they now are, and the nature of their solemn calling. This can take place at this point, or at the sending out at the end of the whole Easter Liturgy. Interestingly, in the American *Book of Common Prayer* (1979) this commissioning is tacked onto the responsorial Apostles' Creed to form a section called 'The Baptismal Covenant', addressed to, and responded to by, the whole assembly, not the candidates. It also comes before the baptism, not after it.

The placement of the Commission in *Common Worship: Times and Seasons* (2006) is far more satisfactory; it follows more naturally after, rather than before, the event, and is brought into far sharper focus by being addressed to the men and women of the moment, the stars of the show, rather than to every Tom, Dick and Harry. However, because the candidates can be excused for feeling a little punch-drunk at this moment, the Commission will have greater impact, and leave a more lasting impression on the candidates and those who witness their initiation, if the option is taken to detach it from the Liturgy of Initiation and place it at the end of the whole shooting match, as the first part of the sending out.

The call to 'continue in the apostles' teaching and fellowship', and among other things to 'persevere' and 'proclaim' will thus resound in their ears and lodge in their hearts and minds as they step forth into the full daylight of Christ's life and power.

Assuming the commission will take place at the end, we move directly from initiation (whether baptism and confirmation or baptism alone) to welcome and acclamation. The president leads the newly initiated, all vested in albs, to the centre of the liturgical space, or to the chancel steps or some other destination point in the space, and shows them to the assembly. President and assembly say the sentence and response of welcome, and applause and cheering break out, with bells and percussion again to the fore.

This concludes the Liturgy of Initiation, but by having moved into the center of the space for the Welcome, the president and the whole assembly are well placed for the sharing of the Peace which immediately follows.

The Liturgy of the Eucharist

At the Easter Liturgy, more than at any other gathering of the people of God, the ability of the assembly to move forward freely as a body to encircle the altar table assumes overriding importance.

Easter Liturgy: the Liturgy of the Eucharist

Having gathered outside around the new fire, having moved through the darkness in growing expectation, and having witnessed the adding of new members to their company, the assembly now moves on again, to their final liturgical destination: the altar table which, as it were, has two legs on earth and two in heaven.

Here the people of God are fed with holy food in the here and now, which they can touch and taste, but at the same time they savour a foretaste of the heavenly banquet for which invitations have arrived but which is still some way off, though eagerly looked forward to. To encourage a real sense of this completion of the journey, at least for now, the space must allow not just a gesture, and indication, of movement, but an actual journey by the whole community, every one of them. There is no place here for first- and second-class worshippers; all must be included in the journey and the expectant crowding around.

In most church buildings with a traditional nave and chancel layout, this is likely to be achieved by clearing the chancel of choir stalls, placing the altar in the middle, and jamming everyone into the resultant space. Alternatively pews may be cleared from the crossing or the front of the nave to achieve a similar place of gathering around the altar table.

Where this is found to be impossible, recourse should be made to moving to another space altogether – most probably the church hall – to which the assembly processes in true celebratory style (most likely waking a few of the neighbours in the process). In this second liturgical room all that is needed is an empty space for people to stand, with an altar table set in the middle. Here the assembly can offer together the Liturgy of the Eucharist and then move immediately into breakfast. However it is achieved, at the Easter Liturgy, journey should trump all other considerations.

The remainder of the Liturgy of the Eucharist on Easter morning follows very much the regular pattern, until after the Communion, when there is a choice to be made concerning the location of the assembly for the concluding stages of the Liturgy.

With a large crowd, some of whom may be one-off or occasional participants, and after a lengthy act of worship, it is probably pushing our luck to try to move the assembly back to their places for a period of reflection. By this time the kids are getting fractious, and the not-so-young can smell the coffee, and it's time to move things along. On this occasion, therefore, after the final communion song and with the assembly still standing around the altar table, the president should move directly to the post-communion prayer, and then into the sending out.

The sending out

At the sending out, the president should first call forth the newly baptized and/or confirmed to stand in the midst of the assembly. Each of the newly initiated is given a lighted candle, using the words said by president and people on page 371 of *Common Worship: Times and Seasons* (2006). This is a far more helpful place for this ceremony than immediately after baptism, when the poor candidate is given a naked flame just before being enveloped by a congratulatory crowd.

The Commission (p. 347 or 366) is then pronounced, which quite fittingly brings back into focus the centrality of Christian initiation to the whole rite. We rejoice at this evidence of new life bursting forth in our community of faith, and we are encouraged once again to gird our loins for the rough and tumble of daily life. Where no Liturgy of Initiation has taken place, the Commission should be used by the whole assembly, just to keep us on our toes. As mentioned before, the option exists for everyone to relight their candles at this point, but by this time half of them won't know where their candles are, and the time-consuming business of passing the flame will appear fiddly and a distraction from our main purpose.

If the Commission is used at this point of sending out, the striking words of each sentence, lifted and given force by the excited voices of our fellow pilgrims with whom we stand shoulder to shoulder, will thus resound in our ears as we go forth from this life-changing experience of worship which has one foot in heaven but one foot very much in the here and now. All present at this Easter celebration will thereby be reminded that, amidst the warm feelings and the rosy glow, we have work still to do.

At the conclusion of the rite the special Easter blessing(s) is pronounced by the president, and here we find ourselves spoilt for choice. In addition to that lovely old favourite from BCP days exulting that God has 'brought again from the dead our Lord Jesus, that great shepherd of the sheep', we have also available the contemporary reworking of the fourfold blessings, the rhythm of which gives them a particular power and resonance.

The dismissal includes a brace of Alleluias which, depending on the capabilities of the deacon, or cantor, or assembly, one can go to town on in various ways. If in doubt, that glorious standby, classic understatement, will also do very nicely.

After such a liturgy, no one of course should be allowed to go home or slink away. The whole assembly should *dance* its way to the breakfast, accompanied by musicians with a good sense of rhythm, appropriate instruments to give the beat, and sufficiently extrovert to teach a few basic steps before we set off. This is no time to be coy.

Music for Easter (Easter Vigil)

See Appendix 3 for full publishing details.

At the lighting of the candles

'Kindle a flame', Iona Community, in *Ritual Song*.

Exsultet

Response

'I want to walk as a child of the light', Kathleen Thomerson, in *The Hymnal 1982*.

First reading with choral response

'Genesis: a reading for the Easter Vigil', Edward Nowak, GIA Publications (sheet music).

Psalm after the first reading

Psalm 136, G. Elvey, H. W. Davies, G. Thalben-Ball, in *The Anglican Chant Psalter*.

Psalm after the second reading

Psalm 16: 'You will show me the path of life', Scott Soper, in *Singing the Psalms* and *Breaking Bread Hymnal*.

Psalm after the third reading

Canticle 8, plainchant, in *The Hymnal 1982*.

Psalm after the fourth reading

Psalm 42: 'As the deer pants for the water', Martin Nystrom, in *Complete Anglican Hymns Old & New*.

Psalm after the fifth reading

Psalm 98: 'All the ends of the earth', Rosalie Bonighton, in *Sunday Psalms*.

The great Easter fanfare

The great Easter fanfare, in *The Hymnal 1982*.

Gloria

'Gloria', William Matthias, in *The Hymnal 1982*.

Gospel acclamation

Alleluia in C (7/8), Howard Hughes, in *The Hymnal 1982*.

Litany of the saints

'Litany of the saints', John D. Becker, in *Breaking Bread Hymnal*.

Sprinkling song

'O Blessed Spring' (tune: 'Berglund'), Robert Buckley Farlee, in *Wonder, Love and Praise*.

Song of journey (to the altar table)

'This joyful Eastertide', Vruechten, in *The Hymnal 1982*.

Communion song

Choral anthem, 'The Easter Song of Praise', Richard Shephard, in *Ash Wednesday to Easter for Choirs*.
'We walk by faith' (tune: 'Shanti'), Marty Haugen, in *Gather* and *The Complete Celebration Hymnal*.

Closing hymn

'Jesus Christ is risen today' (tune: 'Easter Hymn'), in *The Hymnal 1982*.

Sending Out

'Thank you, Lord', in *Lift Every Voice and Sing*.

Communal dance

Other options for Easter worship

The notes above have concentrated on the full-blown Easter Liturgy celebrated by a faith community as its main Easter service in the setting of the building(s) in which it assembles week by week.

There will be many other situations where pastoral or evangelistic needs demand a more selective and creative use of the liturgical material at the Church's disposal. As is so often the case, spontaneous liturgical combustion occurs in all kinds of least-expected places, a phenomenon best explained as a work of the Holy Spirit knocking our heads together.

Dawn services, for example, whenever pooh-poohed by traditional liturgists as totally unworkable, immediately spring up on hilltops overlooking every major city, organized by Christian groups with allegedly zero liturgical awareness. The connection between sunrise and Son rise (what a revelation!) is made anew in people's minds, the crowds turn out, and the stiff-necked mainstream is once again left standing.

Common Worship: Times and Seasons (2006, p. 398) is ahead of the curve here, suggesting ways in which local churches can take a fresh look at whatever natural feature is readily available in the neighborhood – hilltop, river, garden, cave – and use that as a starting point for an Easter celebration that begins where people are and with what they have at their disposal.

Easter liturgies such as these will be inevitably ad hoc and cobbled together, but will have in common a willingness to use whatever natural feature is available and easily recognizable in the life of the local community as a starting point, drawing out the significance of the feature in the Easter story in order to plant its meaning and power in the humdrum reality of everyday existence.

Depending on the situation, different elements of the full Easter Liturgy can be emphasized in order to make the connection between various aspects of the Easter story and what is there before people's eyes. Given a hilltop situation, the Golgotha of our night can be seen as dawn breaks to be the mount of transfiguration where the glorified Christ is revealed; at a riverside, the connection can be made between Christian initiation and reaffirmation today and Jesus' own anointing in baptism at a river bank at the outset of his ministry and his going up to Jerusalem. Outside an 'all-day breakfast' truck stop on the by-pass, we find our own Emmaus, where the Risen Lord makes himself known to us in the breaking of the bread.

It will take just a little imagination, though perhaps a larger dose of pastoral sensitivity and liturgical style, to take elements from all four constituent parts of the Easter Liturgy and weave them into an Easter celebration to fit an unusual venue or particular circumstances.

Vesture will be simple – probably just an alb and a stole – as will language and gesture. The greatest care needs to be taken with music; either going to considerable trouble to support music outdoors with appropriate instruments and adequate amplification, or cutting out music altogether. What should be avoided at all costs is the experience of half-hearted singing lost in the wind, a sure way to convince participants that this is a disorganized outfit lacking confidence and expertise.

All this requires of a faith community an awareness of its cultural context, and a finger on the pulse of the local community, with an openness to try new ideas and new places.

8 EASTERTIDE

Eastertide: the assembly gathered around the ambo

Historical background

From the beginning the Church sustained for a period of 50 days its rejoicing at the new dawn of the era of the Risen Christ. Originally the whole of this period was called Pentecost, although that name is now applied only to the feast which concludes Eastertide, seven weeks after Easter Day itself.

This 50-day period following the feast of the resurrection was a time of great joy and triumph for the Church, and we note that kneeling and fasting both were outlawed for this prolonged period of celebration (oh that we could do likewise, and banish traffic jams at our altar rails for evermore).

Given the propensity of the Church for converting and baptizing pagan usage for Christian purposes, it should come as no surprise to learn that the most likely source of the name, according to Bede in the seventh century, is 'Eostre', the name of an Anglo-Saxon goddess of spring and fertility (as in oestrogen). Even though there is no supporting evidence for the existence of such a goddess, it nevertheless looks as if the Easter festival simply appropriated an earlier pagan one celebrated at the same time of year. Customs such as Easter eggs and hot cross buns are probably pagan in origin, and the Christian explanations of their significance displaced the original connection to the new life of spring and the quarters of the moon.

Over time, the Church's well-developed rituals and customs in celebration of the resurrection of Christ have buried the original pagan antecedents as deeply as a mafioso's victim in a New Jersey construction site.

Cultural context

In today's culture of instant gratification, clergy find themselves fighting a constant battle to remind congregations that Easter is a season, not a day. However, the Church's observance of the Easter season, exhibiting certain liturgical features that distinguish Eastertide from other seasons, help us keep the party spirit going.

Choreography

The Easter Candle is lit at every principal service throughout the season, and remains in a prominent location, most fittingly near the ambo, until moved to the font when Eastertide is over; alleluias are interspersed liberally throughout the liturgies of Eastertide; white or gold vestments are worn throughout the season; and in the liturgical calendar the celebration of Easter rules the roost, not only on Sundays, but also displacing on weekdays all commemorations of saints except for major festivals of apostles or, in some years, of the annunciation.

Seasonal artwork can also play an important part in striking a different visual note in the liturgical space, especially if large and bold enough to dominate the space. During Eastertide 2007, for example, Gerard di Falco's triptych *Triune Resurrection*

Art for Eastertide Philadelphia 2008: 'Finding Surface' by Angela Victor

was hung at the east end of Philadelphia Cathedral, its rich colouring reinforcing the celebratory mood of the season.

It will be appropriate during Eastertide for the liturgical ministers to enter in procession, and for the penitential rite to be replaced by the Gloria or other song of praise. The assembly moves to the font after the Liturgy of the Word, rather than at the beginning, and there makes an affirmation of faith, and is sprinkled. The prayers of the people then follow, and the sharing of the Peace, before the assembly moves to the altar table.

Liturgical texts both old and new enrich the season. A particular treasure of the Anglican tradition are the Easter Anthems, beginning, 'Christ our Passover has been sacrificed for us, so let us celebrate the feast.' They are a compilation of key resurrection texts of great poetic power drawn from 1 Corinthians and Romans. They date in their present form from the Book of Common Prayer (1662), although they first appeared minus the opening passage from 1 Corinthians 5.7b, 8 in the Book of Common Prayer (1549).

The stations of the resurrection (*Common Worship: Times and Seasons* (2006, pp. 443–68) are by contrast a very recent development, emerging it is thought from

Spain and Portugal in the last fifty years. They mirror the more familiar stations of the cross, but this time the stations take us on a journey of joyful encounter with the Risen Lord.

The stations of the resurrection provide up to 19 stations, each focused on a personal encounter with the Risen Christ as described in the Gospels and Acts. They form a valuable resource and a useful tool for punctuating the 50 days with something fresh and spiritually stimulating, in a season when otherwise our liturgical energy may begin to flag a little.

As we move from station to station, enriched perhaps by prints of some of the classical representations in art of many of these Gospel accounts, this devotion helps us reflect upon, and appropriate for ourselves, the mystery of these encounters with he who was killed yet lives among us. They demand silence and space as well as story and visual stimuli.

If gathering a congregation during the week is problematic, the stations of the resurrection might usefully form the Liturgy of the Word of the principal eucharistic celebration one Sunday in Eastertide. Obviously this use of the stations mustn't be overdone, else the rhythm of the lectionary would be lost, but they might well be used on say Easter 2, a Sunday (notorious in clergy folklore as 'sag Sunday') which sometimes needs a pick-me-up

See-at-a-glance Liturgy of Eastertide

Chair

Entrance – processional hymn
Greeting
Song of praise

Ambo

Prayer of the day
Reading from Hebrew Scriptures
Psalm
Reading from Christian Scriptures
Alleluia
Gospel
Procession of Gospel Book

Homily

Silence

Song of journey

Font

Affirmation of faith
Prayers of the people

The Peace
Song of journey

Altar table

Song of offering
The eucharistic prayer
Sanctus
Lord's Prayer
Fraction
Communion
Invitation to reflection

Ambo

Silence

Song of reflection
Post-communion prayer
Announcements
Sending out

Music for Sunday Liturgy in Eastertide

See Appendix 3 for full publishing details

Entrance song

'That Easter day with joy was bright' (tune: 'Puer Nobis'), in *The Hymnal 1982*.

Song of praise

'My soul rejoices', Owen Alstott, in *Celebration Hymnal for Everyone* and *Breaking Bread Hymnal*.

Psalm

Psalm 118, Riyehee Hong, www.riyehee.com

Gospel acclamation

'Joyful Alleluia', Howard Hughes, in *Gather*.

Song of journey (to the font)

'I come with joy' (tune: 'Land of rest'), American folk tune, in *The Hymnal 1982*.

Sprinkling song

'We praise you God' (tune: 'Marsh Chapel'), Max Miller, in *Wonder, Love and Praise*.

Song of journey (to the altar table)

'Led like a lamb', Graham Kendrick, in *Complete Anglican Hymns Old & New*.

Song of offering

'Take O take me as I am', John L. Bell, in *Evangelical Lutheran Worship*.

Communion song

'Come my Way, my Truth, my Life' (tune: 'The call', Ralph Vaughan Williams), in *The Hymnal 1982* and *New Hymns and Worship Songs*.

Song of reflection

'One is the body' (tune: 'Peacock'), John L. Bell, in *One is the Body*.

ASCENSION DAY

Historical background

Ascension Day celebrates the apotheosis of Jesus the Christ, an event recorded by the common author of the third Gospel and of Acts. Originally an integral part of the celebration of Pentecost, in the latter half of the fourth century it was detached and made a major festival in its own right. It falls always on the fortieth day of Eastertide, the Thursday after Easter 6.

Ascension is a major feast of the Christian year, affirming the exaltation of Christ into the heavenly realm, the completion and culmination of all that he came to do and to be. The notion of ascension or exaltation has its roots in the Judaic tradition, both scriptural, for example the assumption of Elijah (2 Kings 2.11), and legendary, for example the assumption of Moses, and is a popular New Testament theme:

> Therefore it is said,
> 'When he ascended on high he made captivity itself a captive;
> he gave gifts to his people.' (Ephesians 4.8)

Cultural context

Today there is less unalloyed joy at the notion of ascension. Because it commemorates a rather nebulous event recorded in only one of the Gospels, and because it perpetuates a pre-Enlightenment understanding of the physical relationship between earth and heaven, Ascension Day is something of an embarrassment to many Christians today. Preachers find themselves having to do some heavy explaining away. The ascension as historical event demands a simplistic view of heaven as a place 'up there', a destination reached by Jesus travelling on a cloud (Acts 1.9).

The main value of the feast, once we get beyond the crude modelling of the heavenly sphere, lies in the sense of completion, vindication and glorification. The stories that Jesus himself told about sons or servants and loving fathers or just masters can now be applied to himself: 'Well done, good and trustworthy slave' (Matthew 25.21).

Today however, the emphasis on Pentecost, the fiftieth day of Easter, as the true completion of the Easter story makes inevitable to some degree the relegation of Ascension to the fortieth milepost along the Easter way. In this process, one casualty is the character of the ten-day period between Ascension and Pentecost as a period of deprivation and waiting (Jesus gone and the Spirit not yet come). This was a useful insight in terms of pastoral theology as the Church prepared for Pentecost, but its loss can be seen as a trade-off for a greater sense of unity and cohesion throughout the whole 50-day Easter season which we now enjoy.

Choreography

There are very few ceremonies pertaining to Ascension alone, and what few there were have been discontinued. Once upon a time (that is, up to 1970) Ascension Day was the best ever day for a young server with a long reach, for until the liturgical reforms flowing from Vatican II, the Easter Candle was extinguished with great drama immediately following the Gospel on Ascension Day. The smoke from the extinguished candle drifting lazily up into the rafters gave you your very own version of the ascension, right before your eyes. Now, however, the Easter Candle remains lit until Pentecost. Perhaps it's a liturgical case of 'from those who have nothing, even what they have will be taken away' (Matthew 13.12).

PENTECOST

The coming of the Spirit of God, the promised gift of Jesus the Christ, upon the Church is the crowning glory of the Easter story, 50 days on from the resurrection. It can be seen as the birthday of the Church.

Historical background

Pentecost (literally 'fiftieth' in the Greek) takes its name from the fiftieth day of the Jewish Feast of Weeks, a pilgrim festival which stretched for 50 days from Passover. The descent of the Spirit described in Acts 2 just happened to take place on this Jewish holiday, the name of which was thereafter appropriated by the Christian Church to denote all things associated with the celebration of the Spirit's presence and power and, in later centuries, of the churches which sprang up energized by an emphasis on life in the Spirit (had it all occurred on August Bank Holiday Monday, Pentecostalists might now be called Augustans).

The Christian version of Pentecost has experienced some shrinkage with the passage of time. At the very beginning, Pentecost was the name given to the whole 50-day period we now refer to as Eastertide, a time of great joy and triumph, originally a festival which combined commemoration of both the ascension of Christ and the descent of the Holy Spirit. During the fourth century, however, this unitive feast was dismantled in favour of two distinct commemorations. Pentecost thereafter became associated solely with the Spirit's coming upon the Church.

Cultural context

Due largely to the influence, albeit unrecognized, of the Renewal (or Charismatic) Movement of the 1960s, there is today a wider acceptance of the notion that at Pentecost the Holy Spirit should be let out of the cage, at least for a day, even if exercised within well-defined boundaries.

Many parishes today, for example, are perfectly at home with a time during or immediately following the eucharist when prayers for the sick can be offered, with laying on of hands and anointing. At Pentecost the compass of such prayer ministry is often extended to embrace personal needs of a more spiritual nature such as opening oneself to the gifts of the Spirit or surrendering one's life to God anew.

The Liturgy of Pentecost has therefore gradually come to include a heightened degree of awareness of the life of the Spirit and expectation of the Spirit's potential for breaking through our barriers and disturbing and changing our lives. This is nothing new, or non-liturgical (remember Richard Meux Benson and his eschatological mass), but it is now more general and unexceptional. We arrive in the narthex before the eucharist, on any Sunday but especially on Pentecost, as we would arrive to check in at an airport for a surprise holiday; not sure of our destination, but excited to be there.

Choreography

Apart from the rich liturgical texts and scriptural readings which abound on the theme of the Spirit, there are no particular liturgical ceremonies marking the feast of Pentecost. The Easter Candle, standing in the midst of the assembly for the whole 50 days, will be lit for the last time at Pentecost before being moved to stand by the baptismal font for the rest of the year (where it is lit only for Liturgies of Initiation), but there is no theatrical extinguishing of the Candle as in the old days at Ascension.

So Pentecost is very much a case of 'over to you'. Given the wondrous promises of Jesus concerning the life of the coming Spirit, and all those dramatic stories from the Acts of the Apostles chronicling the Spirit's intervention in the experience of the first followers of the Way, how might we enliven the worship of the eucharistic assembly on this day? How might the Holy Spirit be transformed from a theological abstract into a living being that demands of us response?

Creative minds have a field day at Pentecost, and it can be fun to let loose on this day those in our community who are gifted with thematic learning. Whether it's white paper doves released from a net in the rafters during the liturgy, or red helium balloons released in the street afterwards, there are endless ways of bringing to life the themes of this day, and we should enjoy exploring them.

Pentecost: banner at Kamloops Cathedral, British Columbia

The Pentecost scene described in Acts 2.1–13 focuses on the many languages in which the message was heard, and this can be reproduced fairly easily in most congregations today, given the multicultural world we inhabit. Care should be taken to avoid a line-up at the ambo of all the different language-speakers waiting in turn to repeat the same passage; this will induce sleep rather than excitement. Instead, creative minds should invent ways in which different languages may be heard without lengthening the readings to any unacceptable degree.

Where the ministry of the laying on of hands with anointing is to take place, this should be done within the context of the liturgy, and every effort should be made to avoid giving the impression that this is a hole-in-the-corner job for those so inclined. On the feast of Pentecost particularly, it is essential that, wherever this ministry takes place, it is seen to be integral to the worship of the whole assembly.

At the same time the ministry of the laying on of hands should be devised in such a way that those not taking part nevertheless feel involved; not just left to kick their heels but asked to participate at least by prayer. Care should be taken to ensure that sufficient ministers are available to avoid unnecessary delay, and the president should explain beforehand the shape and purpose of the ministry in such a way that those not going forward to be prayed with feel themselves to be participants just as much as those who do. The help of all those present should be called forth.

This ministry is best organized following communion, when the period of songs and other music can easily be extended or shortened to suit the circumstances. Because the gift of healing, and other like charisms, are not the exclusive preserve of the clergy, and can be manifested at the hands of the least likely of candidates, it is important to blur the edges a little.

While the clergy will of course be involved, so too will others: members of prayer or healing groups, those who have a track record in this field, or simply those who have a caring pastoral spirit. The pastor must take the trouble to set up everything with clear guidelines and expectations, and with as little confusion as possible about who is doing what, and why. The criteria for being asked to minister to others should be easily understood by all.

THE FEAST OF THE TRANSFIGURATION

This is the celebration of the remarkable event in Christ's life, recorded in all three Synoptic Gospels when, in the company of Peter, James and John on a high mountain, 'he was transfigured before them, and his face shone like the sun' (Matthew 17.2).

Historical background

It is puzzling that such a well-recorded and significant event in the life of Christ should have had to struggle so long for recognition. It is of the highest significance theologically, in that not only is Christ's glory revealed momentarily during his earthly life, but his relationship to Jewish Law and the prophets is spelt out by the appearance of Moses and Elijah.

Perhaps the early Church knew something we don't (certainly there is something awfully convenient about this neat line-up of leading characters), or perhaps (as some scholars now assert) this was a resurrection appearance that somehow got lost or which was hijacked by the gospel authors for their own ends as storytellers.

In any event, it was not until 1000 CE that the feast is widely spoken of in the East, and even later in the West. The date of the transfiguration has prosaic origins in that when Pope Callistus III ordered the general observance of the feast in 1457 in commemoration of a great victory over the Turks, he chose 6 August simply because the good news had reached Rome on that day.

This accident of history has rather left the transfiguration hung out to dry, unrelated to the rest of the cycle of liturgical feasts marking the major events in Christ's life.

Cultural context

By a weird coincidence, 6 August marks also the transfiguration of our world by dint of humankind's harnessing nuclear power to destructive ends. On 6 August 1945 the first atomic bomb was unleashed upon the Japanese city of Hiroshima, and ever after the world has had to live with the threat of nuclear holocaust. It is a bizarre pair of co-ordinates, the irony of which would no doubt have been lost on Harry S. Truman who, although one of America's greatest presidents, would have had other things on his mind than the liturgical calendar during those awful days.

Once again, the Church is given an opportunity to tap into major concerns in contemporary society. There is widespread horror at weapons of mass destruction, and readiness on the part of significant numbers of people to attend peace vigils and marches to register their concern.

Choreography

These two strands of meaning of transfiguration, one glorious one terrifying, provide the jumping-off point for any Liturgy of Transfiguration Day.

The liturgy should be advertised as a day when both strands will be honoured: the rite will be celebratory, in the light of all that Christ is for humankind, and penitential, as we reflect on our desecration of creation and our abuse of God-given knowledge and skill.

An evening liturgy might begin at a venue other than the place of liturgical celebration, where local leaders of the peace movement or nuclear disarmament organization address the assembly on the significance of this day for humanity. The assembly then processes to the church building or other suitable venue for a liturgy focusing on the transfiguration of Christ. If this is to engage those not normally found in church, it must be stripped to the bare bone, and include readings from sources other than the Scriptures alone.

9 THE KINGDOM SEASON

The kingdom season does not really exist as a recognized part of the Church's Year, but may be said to be an emergent season likely to gain ground as time passes. It covers the period between All Saints' Day and Advent, and culminates, in terms of Sunday worship, in the feast of Christ the King.

The kingdom season is not found in *Common Worship: Times and Seasons* (2006) but is referred to in the highly regarded *Celebrating Common Prayer* (2002), an inspired publication, based largely on the office book of the Anglican Franciscans. David Stancliffe (at that time Chair of the Liturgical Commission) and Br Tristam of the Society of St Francis were the prime movers. Even here, however, the kingdom season is referred to *en passant* rather than as an official title for the period in question.

The way for a kingdom season was prepared by the *Alternative Service Book 1980*, which covered the same period with nine 'Sundays before Christmas'. The first five of these were subtitled 'Sundays before Advent', and the last four were named Sundays in Advent, subtitled Sundays before Christmas. Christ the King was ignored (1980 already seems a long time ago). This was always confusing, however, and cannot be seen as an encouraging start. It was never going to work, launching the Church's Year way out on the formless liturgical sea at an arbitrary point called 'The Ninth Sunday before Christmas', some time in early November. The compilers of the ASB had obviously never done a basic marketing course.

Common Worship (2000) is more modest in its aims for this period of the year. It provides four 'Sundays before Advent' (and is not shy of calling the last of these 'Christ the King'), but these are clearly seen as the last of the old year, not the first of the new. This saves all the subtitling, and deals more creatively with the conflicted nature of these four Sundays in liturgical no-man's land.

The conflicted nature of the kingdom season arises from its tending to look both backwards and forwards at the same time. It needs both to meet the natural desire for a change after the interminable weeks of Ordinary Time, and the gathering pace of expectation at this time of year in secular culture, but at the same time avoid the appearance of a preparation for the preparation (Advent).

Faced with this quandary, *Common Worship* (2000) did the best it could, and plumped for a season which recapitulates all that has gone before, celebrates the primary themes of the kingdom of God, and brings everything to a glorious climax on the final Sunday of the liturgical year with the feast of Christ the King.

What does the kingdom season have to say? Well, the propers and the readings for these Sundays of the kingdom season stake out the ground.

The collects focus on themes of restoration and glory: the first lifts up the 'faith and power of love' of the saints (in the aftermath of All Saints' Day); the second proclaims our Lord as 'the king of all' in whom God will restore all things; the third looks to Christ's appearing in 'power and great glory', and the fourth (Christ the King) acclaims Christ 'ascended to the throne of heaven'.

The readings in the three-year cycle of the Revised Common Lectionary concentrate on major themes of the coming kingdom of God, whether seen in the dramatic events that will usher in the end time, or the abandonment of self in pursuing the love of God or neighbour. The kingdom is proclaimed, in parable, in proclamation and in teaching. The season could be summarized in the words attributed to Jesus in his charge to the seventy: 'Yet know this: the kingdom of God has come near' (Luke 10.11).

Now that the 'preparation for the preparation' of the *Alternative Service Book 1980* has been abandoned, the kingdom season can be seen for what it is: more green Sundays (therefore technically a continuation of Ordinary Time), but with a quickening of pace from All Saints' Day onwards. Here the Church concludes its yearly liturgical journey by recalling and celebrating all that God has done for us in Christ Jesus as we ponder the mystery of the kingdom which beckons us and yet is among us.

Care should be taken in any alteration to the liturgical space in terms of orientation or seating not to steal the thunder of Advent Sunday, when a more dramatic change will be necessary. It may be possible however to make some changes which will flag up the change of pace in subtle ways, so that a sense of continuity with all that has gone before is maintained.

These Sundays of the kingdom season would be appropriate times for the community of faith to bring to the liturgy tokens of thanksgiving to God for all that has gone before. This could include stewardship renewal of course – the best possible time of the year for this essential part of the renewal of our common life – but also a ceremony in which the assembly presents at the altar table baskets full of their letters to God, listing the many things we thank God for as we take stock of the year.

This time of recapitulation is an appropriate time to emphasize the importance of the sacrament of reconciliation, to teach about it in homily and news-sheet, and to make it available at as many different regular and convenient times as possible.

10 AND FINALLY . . .

This short walk through a typical year in the Church's liturgical life presupposes many things – a group of people desiring to worship, a faithful and creative pastor, a place to meet – but above all, a community of faith open to the possibilities. Without this prerequisite, the patterns of worship described in this book will not spring into life.

By this we mean a congregation ready to become an assembly; an assembly of gifts and skills and ministries, whose members come to the altar table knowing themselves to be God's holy priestly people. They stand in humility and praise, but with heads erect and hands open in offering, exulting in the wondrous truth that they are called, and named and known and cherished:

> We thank you for counting us worthy
> to stand in your presence and serve you.
> (Eucharistic Prayer B, *Common Worship*, 2006)

The ways in which we draw forth ministry and mutual service from within the faith community, realizing thereby the full potential of those alongside whom we journey and worship, is a matter of the highest importance in creating worship that engages, inspires and transforms.

At Philadelphia Cathedral, as at St Thomas' Huddersfield, the way forward has been to disband the various teams of 'experts' – readers, servers, intercessors, sacristans, coffee-makers etc. – and replace them with teams of Jacks and Jills of all trades.

The whole congregation is divided up into teams of between 10 and 15 members, and a different team is on duty each Sunday to 'make the liturgy happen'. The team will cover all the tasks required, from preparing the altar table and the liturgical space, greeting, reading the Scriptures, leading the prayers, presenting the gifts, serving, acting as thurifer, making refreshments, welcome of the newcomer, and clearing away.

The team meets to allocate tasks, and teams join together for training where needed. As they work together a team spirit develops and with it a greater desire to meet in one another's homes, which results in a readiness to deepen faith and grow in discipleship as well as merely performing practical tasks.

Easter Liturgy: the priestly people of God assembled to make eucharist

The leaders of each team exercise a vital ministry in bringing to life the gifts of the assembly, and can provide an invaluable 'council of advice' for the parish priest in the pastoral care of the community.

We are thus reminded that even creative uncommon worship is not an end in itself, but merely the most telling outward expression of an assembly of God's priestly people, touched by the Spirit, and brought to life as a vibrant, loving and effective community in the work of transformation. An assembly not just talking the talk, but walking the walk.

APPENDIX 1
PRAYERS OF THE PEOPLE

The following prayers were written by Lark Hall, a member of the cathedral community at Philadelphia.

For a Sunday in Advent

Philadelphia Cathedral 10 December 2006

Leader's introduction:
The response to our intercessions today is adapted from the opening lines of the Song of Zechariah, the psalmody appointed for today.

Leader:　Blessed are you, Lord, the God of Israel,
People:　**You have come to your people**
　　　　　and set them free.

1　Blessed are you, Lord,
　　the God of Israel,
　　You have come to your people
　　and set them free.

　　It's been a tough week at work –
　　Papers to grade, papers to write, papers to read
　　Clients to see, clients to bill, clients to heal
　　Deadlines to meet, schedules to rearrange, email to delete –

　　But it's the second Sunday of Advent
　　And I'm trying to remember

2   Blessed are you, Lord,
the God of Israel,
**You have come to your people
and set them free.**

It's been a tough week in the world –
New plans for Iraq, old plans for Iraq,
New murders in the local news, old murders in the local news,
School cheating revealed, school budget crisis resolved,
Genocide in Darfur, unrest in the Middle East –

But it's the second Sunday of Advent
And I'm trying to remember

3   Blessed are you, Lord,
the God of Israel,
**You have come to your people
and set them free.**

It's been a tough couple of weeks in the diocese –

A bishop challenged, a bishop elected,
Retired clergy to acknowledge, new clergy to ordain,

Richard having surgery, James improving,
Deidre leaving, Judy staying,
Kris and John joining in

Parishioners with family problems,
Parishioners with new babies
Parishioners with dark doubts
Parishioners with bright joys

Parishioners praying for those in need
(Pause)
Parishioners praying for those who have died
(Pause)

But it's the second Sunday of Advent
And I'm trying to remember

4   Blessed are you, Lord,
the God of Israel,
**You have come to your people
and set them free.**

For Earth Day

Philadelphia Cathedral, April 2001
(inspired by Gail Ramshaw and Gordon Lathrop)

Leader: In honour of Earth Day, let us use for our prayers the words of a familiar
hymn I'm sure you'll all recognize.
Will you join me in the refrain, saying:
Creator God, to thee we raise this our hymn of grateful praise.

For the beauty of the earth, for the beauty of the skies,
For the love which from our birth over and around us lies.
Creator God, to thee we raise this our hymn of grateful praise.

For the beauty of each hour of the day and of the night,
hill and vale, and tree and flower, sun and moon and stars of light.
Creator God, to thee we raise this our hymn of grateful praise.

For the joy of ear and eye, for the heart and mind's delight,
For the mystic harmony linking sense to sound and sight.
Creator God, to thee we raise this our hymn of grateful praise.

For the joy of human love, brother, sister, parent, child,
Friends on earth, and friends above, for all gentle thoughts and mild.
Creator God, to thee we raise this our hymn of grateful praise.

For the Church which evermore lifts up holy hands above
Offering up on every shore your pure sacrifice of love.
Creator God, to thee we raise this our hymn of grateful praise.

A Sunday in Ordinary Time 2002

For our Prayers of the People this morning, let us begin with a short poem by South African writer Alan Paton; then we will add our intercessions.

The response will be: **O Lord, hear our prayer** *(repeat)*

O Lord,
open my eyes that I may see the needs of others; open my ears that I may hear their cries;
open my heart so that they need not be without succour;
let me not be afraid to defend the weak because of the anger of the strong, nor afraid to defend the poor because of the anger of the rich.
Show me where love and hope and faith are needed,
and use me to bring them to those places.
and so open my eyes and my ears
that I may this coming day be able to do some work of peace for thee.

(Source: *United Methodist Hymnal*, 1989, no. 456)

We pray for all who have died,
especially for Joe Fairfax, who was laid to rest this week, and for Inez in her
    bereavement
O Lord, hear our prayer.

We pray for the sick
for those who struggle like Lazarus and for those in any need or trouble, especially
    for Jewel and Father James
O Lord, hear our prayer.

We pray for the church
especially for the Cathedral
and all who serve in any capacity here: seminarians, musicians, volunteers
O Lord, hear our prayer.

We pray for the city, the nation, and the world
For the courage to live in these times, and for the courage to change them
O Lord, hear our prayer. Amen.

For Welcome Sunday, 12 November 2006

Our response today on this Welcome Sunday is: **We welcome you, O Lord** (heartily with a smile)

Into our Cathedral
Into our diocesan convention
Into our voters booths
We welcome you, O Lord

Across our neighbourhoods
Across our county
Across our borders
We welcome you, O Lord

Into our workplaces
Into our classrooms
Into our families
We welcome you, O Lord

Into our priorities
Into our pocketbooks
Into our possibilities
We welcome you, O Lord

Into our songs
Into our prayers
At our table
We welcome you, O Lord

Amen. Amen.

For Christ the King, 21 November 2004

Refrain and first stanza from Jerusalem Bible translation of Psalm 46
   The response is: **We give thanks for these mercies.**

All over the world
he puts an end to wars
he breaks the bow
he snaps the spear
he gives shields to the flames.
We give thanks for these mercies.

All over the world
he works for justice and peace
he offers the branch
he binds the wound
he sends food to those in need.
We give thanks for these mercies.

All over the world
she creates in her own image
she disrupts indifference
she reconciles the different
she blesses every act of doubt and faith.
We give thanks for these mercies.

All over the world
she raises up her saints
she sets them walking among us
she labours along beside them
she leads them on the journey home.
We give thanks for these mercies.

All over the world
God listens to the flock's cry and the shepherd's plea
God speaks through art and music, prayer and preaching
God weaves community from every tribe and language
God holds us in the palm of her hand.
We give thanks for these mercies. Amen.

For a Sunday in Ordinary Time, 24 June 2007

Leader: Our intercessions this morning are based on a poem some of you may know, 'The Waking' by American writer Theodore Roethke. The final lines of every other stanza repeat. I would like you to repeat them with me now:

'I learn by going where I have to go' (*motion: people repeat*)

and

'I wake to sleep, and take my waking slow' (*motion: people repeat*)

After I read the poem, I will add some biddings and will ask you to follow them with one of the lines we practised.

The Waking

I wake to sleep, and take my waking slow.
I feel my fate in what I cannot fear.
I learn by going where I have to go.

We think by feeling. What is there to know?
I hear my being dance from ear to ear:
I wake to sleep, and take my waking slow.

Of those so close beside me, which are you?
God bless the Ground! I shall walk softly there,
And learn by going where I have to go.

Light takes the Tree; but who can tell us how?
The lowly worm climbs up a winding stair;
I wake to sleep, and take my waking slow.

Great Nature has another thing to do
To you and me; so take the lively air,
And, lovely, learn by going where to go.

This shaking keeps me steady. I should know.
What falls away is always. And is near.
I wake to sleep, and take my waking slow;
I learn by going where I have to go.

I ask your prayers for those who cannot fear –
>   for those who lead, for those who follow,
>   for prisoners, for their imprisoners,
>   for refugees, for immigrants

'I learn by going where I have to go' (*motion: people repeat*)

I ask your prayers for those who can dance from ear to ear –
>   for children, for their teachers
>   for the laity, for the clergy (especially for Father Kim)
>   for horn players, for organists

'I wake to sleep, and take my waking slow' (*motion: people repeat*)

I ask your prayers for those so close beside me –
>   for those we know, for those we have yet to meet
>   for the Province of lbadan in Nigeria and our companion diocese of Guatemala
>   for all who are healthy, for all who are unhealthy in body or spirit
>   for Marge, for Ada, for . . . for any others you wish to name aloud or silently
>   (*pause*)

>   for all whose lives have blessed ours, whether they are walking beside us or walking before us
>   for . . .
>   (*pause*)

'I learn by going where I have to go' (*motion: people repeat*)

I ask your prayers for the Tree, for the Light
for the lowly worm, for Great Nature
for the shaking, for the lively air
for what falls away and for what is near

'I wake to sleep, and take my waking slow' (*motion: people repeat*)
Amen.

For Easter 2007

Written by John Tuton of St Martin's, Chestnut Hill, Philadelphia, and a member of the Cathedral Chapter.

Let us pray, responding to each petition to the Lord with the words, **Hear our prayer.**

Lord, the stone that sealed your tomb has rolled away and our grieving has turned to joy. You have left us in body so that your Spirit may live in all of us, and risen so that you may remain with us forever. Just as your immortal love has become untombed, let us cast away the stones that emtomb us in our earthly cares, and rise up, made new through the power of your Holy Spirit.

   Lord of our strength and our salvation
   Hear our prayer.

Lord, in this season of re-creation, open our eyes to the wonder of all your works; the emerging flowers, the soon-to-come warmth of the sun, the birds' morning song and the upturned, trusting faces of our children, as full of promise and purpose as your resurrection. Let us love and respect these treasures and nurture them all to the fullness of life.

   Lord of our bounty and our blessings
   Hear our prayer.

Lord, we pray for those who cannot share the joy of your resurrection today; for the improverished in body or in soul, for those consumed by anger, fear or hatred, and especially for the perpetrators and the victims of war. Remind us, Lord, that we suffer most when the least one of us suffers, and we love you most when we truly love one another.

   Lord of our charity and our compassion
   Hear our prayer.

Let us pray for our whole Church. We pray for our Presiding Bishop Katharine, for our diocesan Bishops Charles and Edward, and for Armando, Bishop in our companion diocese in Guatemala. Today we give thanks for *the parishes of San Marcos, San Juan and La Latividad in our companion diocese of Guatemala.* And, in this Easter moment of renewal and rebirth, let us pray for our worldwide Anglican Communion, riven by discord and threatened with dissolution. Give us the wisdom and willingness to embrace our differences, Lord, and reunite us, in this diocese, this country and abroad, with the healing accord of your holy word.

   Lord of our life shared in your spirit
   Hear our prayer.

Lord, we ask you to be with us as we pray for our nation and its leaders. We ask this especially for those in positions of authority who, through ignorance or by intent, favour the fortunes of the privileged, deny the rights of the oppressed and continue to betray our trust. Roll away their stones of indifference, Lord, and strengthen our voices so that we may speak up for our country and reaffirm the sanctity and honour of its institutions, here and throughout the world.

Lord of all dominion and power
Hear our prayer.

Let us pray for those among us who are troubled in body, mind or spirit. I ask your prayers for the following members and friends of our St Martin's family: *Inez Schweller and Donna Latshaw*. I also ask your prayers for those who have died, especially for all those listed in today's leaflet and held forever in our hearts.

Lord of our everlasting life
Hear our prayer.

And now, either silently or aloud, let us offer our own prayers and thanksgivings.

APPENDIX 2
ABBREVIATED VIGIL READINGS, WITH PARTS FOR DIFFERENT READERS

Genesis 1.1—2.4a The Creation

A reading from the Book of Genesis (words in bold to be spoken by a second reader).

In the beginning when God created the heavens and the earth, the earth was a formless void and darkness covered the face of the deep, while a wind from God swept over the face of the waters. Then God said, '**Let there be light**'; and there was light. And God saw that the light was good; and God separated the light from the darkness. God called the light Day, and the darkness he called Night. And there was evening and there was morning, the first day.

Refrain

And God said, '**Let there be a dome in the midst of the waters, and let it separate the waters from the waters.**' So God made the dome and separated the waters that were under the dome from the waters that were above the dome. And it was so. And there was evening and there was morning, the second day.

Refrain

And God said, '**Let the waters under the sky be gathered together into one place, and let the dry land appear.**' Then God said, '**Let the earth put forth vegetation: plants** yielding seed, and fruit trees of every kind on earth that bear fruit with the seed in it.' And it was so. And God saw that it was good. And there was evening and there was morning, the third day.

Refrain

And God said, '**Let there be lights in the dome of the sky to separate the day from the night; and let them be for signs and for seasons and for days and years, and let them be lights in the dome of the sky to give light upon the earth.**' And it was so. And God saw that it was good. And there was evening and there was morning, the fourth day.

Refrain

And God said, '**Let the waters bring forth swarms of living creatures, and let birds fly above the earth across the dome of the sky.**' So God created every living creature that moves. And God saw that it was good. God blessed them, saying, '**Be fruitful and multiply and fill the waters in the seas, and let birds multiply on the earth.**' And there was evening and there was morning, the fifth day.

Refrain

Then God said, '**Let us make humankind in our image, according to our likeness; and let them have dominion over the fish of the sea, and over the birds of the air, and over the cattle, and over all the wild animals of the earth, and over every creeping thing that creeps upon the earth.**' And it was so. God saw everything that he had made, and indeed, it was very good. And there was evening and there was morning, the sixth day.

Refrain

Thus the heavens and the earth were finished, and all their multitude. And on the seventh day God finished the work that he had done, and he rested on the seventh day from all the work that he had done.

(long pause)

Holy wisdom, holy word.

Genesis 22.1–18 Abraham and Isaac

A reading from the Book of Genesis (words in bold to be spoken by a second reader).

After these things God tested Abraham. He said to him, 'Abraham!' And he said, 'Here I am.' He said, '**Take your son, your only son Isaac, whom you love, and go to the land of Moriah, and offer him there as a burnt-offering on one of the mountains that I shall show you.**'

So Abraham rose early in the morning, saddled his donkey, and took two of his young men with him, and his son Isaac; he cut the wood for the burnt-offering, and set out and went to the place in the distance that God had shown him. Abraham took the wood of the burnt-offering and laid it on his son Isaac, and he himself carried the fire and the knife.

When they came to the place that God had shown him, Abraham built an altar there and laid the wood in order. He bound his son Isaac, and laid him on the altar, on top of the wood. Then Abraham reached out his hand and took the knife to kill his son.

But the angel of the LORD called to him from heaven, and said, 'Abraham, Abraham!' And he said, 'Here I am.' He said, '**Do not lay your hand on the boy or do anything to him; for now I know that you fear God, since you have not withheld your son, your only son, from me.**'

The angel of the LORD called to Abraham a second time from heaven, and said, '**By myself I have sworn, says the LORD: Because you have done this, and have not withheld your son, your only son, I will indeed bless you, and I will make your offspring as numerous as the stars of heaven and as the sand that is on the seashore. And your offspring shall possess the gate of their enemies, and by your offspring shall all the nations of the earth gain blessing for themselves, because you have obeyed my voice.**'

(*long pause*)

Holy wisdom, holy word.

Exodus 14.10—15.1a Crossing the Read Sea

A reading from the Book of Exodus (words in bold to be spoken by a second reader).

As Pharaoh drew near, the Israelites looked back, and there were the Egyptians advancing on them. In great fear the Israelites cried out to the LORD. But Moses said to the people, 'Do not be afraid, stand firm, and see the deliverance that the LORD will accomplish for you today; for the Egyptians whom you see today you shall never see again.'

Then the LORD said to Moses, **'Why do you cry out to me? Tell the Israelites to go forward. But you lift up your staff, and stretch out your hand over the sea and divide it, that the Israelites may go into the sea on dry ground.'**

Then Moses stretched out his hand over the sea. The LORD drove the sea back by a strong east wind all night, and turned the sea into dry land; and the waters were divided. The Israelites went into the sea on dry ground, the waters forming a wall for them on their right and on their left.

At the morning watch the LORD in the pillar of fire and cloud looked down upon the Egyptian army, and threw the Egyptian army into panic. The waters returned and covered the chariots and the chariot drivers, the entire army of Pharaoh that had followed them into the sea; not one of them remained.

But the Israelites walked on dry ground through the sea, the waters forming a wall for them on their right and on their left. Thus the LORD saved Israel that day from the Egyptians; so the people feared the LORD and believed in the LORD and in his servant Moses.

Then Moses and the Israelites sang this song to the LORD: 'I will sing to the LORD, for he has triumphed gloriously; horse and rider he has thrown into the sea.'

(*long pause*)

Holy wisdom, holy word.

APPENDIX 3
MUSIC RESOURCES

We are blessed to live in a time where liturgical music is unlimited. The music in this book is a seasonal selection from hymnals, choral collections for liturgy, and psalms. It represents just the tip of the iceberg of the abundance of musical resources available. It is our duty to be creative in finding music that enhances and encourages our contemporary liturgy. Of course music should reflect a community's culture and history, as well as the liturgy itself, but we should not limit ourselves in these given factors, but aim to liberate our musical experience.

For more information about musical resources for liturgy visit *www.riyehee.com*. To obtain the music visit *www.riyehee.com* or *www.sibeliusmusic.com*.

Hymnal and choral collection

The Addington Service, Royal School of Church Music, 1973.

Advent for Choirs, edited by Malcolm Archer and Stephen Cleobury, Oxford University Press, 2000.

All are Welcome, GIA Publications, Chicago, IL, 1995.

Ash Wednesday to Easter for Choirs, edited by Lionel Dakers and John Scott, Oxford University Press, 1998.

Beneath the Tree of Life, GIA Publications, Chicago, IL, 2000.

Benedictine Book of Song II, The Liturgical Press, Collegeville, MN, 1973.

Be Still and Know: Chants, Songs and Hymns for Contemplative Worship, edited by Margaret Rizza, Kevin Mayhew Ltd, Stowmarket, 2000.

Breaking Bread Hymnal, OCP Publications, Portland, OR, 2006.

Cantate: A Book of Short Chants, Hymns, Responses and Litanies, edited by Stephen Dean, Decani Music Ltd, Brandon, 2005.

Celebration Hymnal for Everyone, I & II, McCrimmons Publishing Co. Ltd, Great Wakering, 1994.

Come All You People: Shorter Songs for Worship, John L. Bell, GIA Publications, Chicago, IL, 1994.

Common Praise – Anglican Church of Canada, Anglican Book Centre, Toronto, 1998.

Complete Anglican Hymns Old & New, Kevin Mayhew Ltd, Stowmarket, 2000.

The Complete Celebration Hymnal, with New Songs of Celebration, McCrimmons Publishing Co. Ltd, Great Wakering, 1991.

Evangelical Lutheran Worship, Augsburg Fortress, Minneapolis, MN, 2006.

Gather, GIA Publications, Chicago, IL, 1994.

Glory & Praise, OCP Publications, Portland, OR, 1998.

Gregorian Missal for Sundays, Monks of Solesmes, Paraclete Press, 1990.

Heaven Shall Not Wait, John L. Bell and Graham Maule, GIA Publications, Chicago, IL, 1989.

Hymnal for the Hours, GIA Publications, Chicago, IL, 1989.

The Hymnal 1982, The Church House Fund, New York, 1985.

Hymns Ancient & Modern Revised, Canterbury Press, London, 2005.

Journeysongs, OCP publications, 1994.

Lectionary Psalms, Grail/Gelineau, GIA Publications, Chicago, IL, 1999.

Lift Every Voice and Sing: An African American Hymnal, The Church Hymnal Corporation, New York, 1993.

The New Church Anthem Book, Oxford University Press, 1994.

The New English Hymnal, Canterbury Press, London, 2002.

New Hymns and Worship Songs – Supplementary Collection, Kevin Mayhew Ltd, Stowmarket, 2001.

One is the Body: Songs of Unity and Diversity, John L. Bell, GIA Publications, Chicago, IL, 2002.

Psallite: Sacred Song for Liturgy and Life, The Collegeville Composers Group, Liturgical Press, Collegeville, MN, 2006.

Ritual Moments: Music for Sacraments, RCIA and Other Occasions, GIA Publications, Chicago, IL, 2005.

Ritual Song: A Hymnal and Service Book for Roman Catholics, GIA Publications, Chicago, IL, 1996.

Wonder, Love and Praise, Church Publishing Inc., New York, 1997.

Sheet music

'The Addington Service – Music for Holy Communion', Order One, RSCM, London, 2002.

'Festival Allelulia', James Ohepponis, Morning Star Publishers, Fenton, MO, 1999.

'Genesis', Edward Nowak, GIA Publications, Chicago, IL, 1990.

'In the Day of the Lord', M. D. Ridge, OCP Publications, Portland, OR, 1992.

'The Love of God Comes Close', John L. Bell and G. Maule, Wild Goose Publications, Glasgow, 1997.

'My God, My God', Liam Lawton, GIA Publications, Chicago, IL, 1993.

'Nunc Dimittis', Christopher Walker, OCP Publications, Portland, OR, 1989.

'O Blessed Spring', Robert Buckley Farlee, Augsburg Fortress, Minneapolis, MN, 1997.

'Praise To You, O Christ, Our Savior', Bernadette Farrell, OCP Publications, Portland, OR, 1986.

'There is something holy here' (Octavo), Christopher Walker, OCP Publications, Portland, OR, 1989.

Psalm settings

The Anglican Chant Psalter, Church Publishing Inc., New York, 1987.

A Hymn Tune Psalter, Book One, Carl P. Daw, Jr. and Kevin R. Hackett, Church Publishing Inc., New York, 1998.

The Ionian Psalter, Peter R. Hallock, edited by Carl Crosier, Ionian Arts, Washington, 1987.

Lectionary Psalms, Grail/Gelineau, GIA Publications, Chicago, IL, 1998.

Psalms for the People, compiled by Norman Warren, Kevin Mayhew Ltd, Stowmarket, 2002.

Singing the Psalms, vols 1, 2, 3 and 4, OCP Publications, Portland, OR, 1997.

Sunday Psalms: Musical Settings for Common Worship, Kevin Mayhew Ltd, Stowmarket, 2000.

SELECT BIBLIOGRAPHY

Alternative Service Book 1980, Clowes, SPCK, Cambridge University Press, Hodder & Stoughton, Oxford University Press, Mowbray.

Beeson, T. 2002. *The Bishops*, London: SCM Press.

Beeson, T. 2006. *The Canons*, London: SCM Press.

Bell, G. K. A. 1952. *Randall Davidson*, London: Oxford University Press.

Bell, J. 1998. *Ritual Song*, GIA Publications.

Book of Common Prayer. 1979. New York: Seabury Press.

Book of Occasional Services. 2000. New York: Church Publishing.

Brind, J. and Wilkinson, T. 2004. *Crafts for Creative Worship*, London: Canterbury Press.

Celebrating Common Prayer. 2002. London: Continuum.

Common Worship: Services and Prayers for the Church of England. 2000. London: Church House Publishing.

Common Worship: Christian Initiation. 2006. London: Church House Publishing.

Common Worship: Times and Seasons. 2006. London: Church House Publishing.

Davies, J. G. (ed.). 1986. *A New Dictionary of Liturgy and Worship*, London: SCM Press.

Doll, P. 2005. *Liturgy and Architecture for a Pilgrim People*, London: Affirming Catholicism.

Giles, R. 2004a. *Creating Uncommon Worship: Transforming the Liturgy of the Eucharist*, London: Canterbury Press; Collegeville, MN: Liturgical Press (2005).

Giles, R. 2004b. *Re-Pitching the Tent: Reordering the Church Building for Worship and Mission (revised and expanded edition)*, London: Canterbury Press; Collegeville, MN: Liturgical Press (2004).

Henson, H. 1946. *Retrospect of an Unimportant Life*, London: Oxford University Press.

The Hymnal 1982, New York: Church Publishing.

International Commission on English in the Liturgy. 2001. *Opening Prayers: Collects in Contemporary Language*, London: Canterbury Press.

Lent, Holy Week and Easter. 1984/1986. London: Church House Publishing/SPCK.

Levitt, J. and Strassfeld. 1950. M. *A Night of Questions: A Passover Haggadah*, Reconstructionist Press.

Lang, U. M. 2004. *Turning Towards the Lord*, San Francisco: Ignatius Press.

Wild Goose Resource Group. 2000. *Cloth for the Cradle: Worship Resources and Readings for Advent, Christmas and Epiphany*, Glasgow: Wild Goose.